W9-AJP-321

Darkness in the Marketplace

The Christian at Prayer in the World

Thomas H. Green, SJ

A Sequel to OPENING TO GOD and
WHEN THE WELL RUNS DRY

Ave Maria Press   Notre Dame, Indiana

Imprimi Potest:
Joaquin G. Bernas, S.J.
Provincial of the Province of the Philippines
January 14, 1981

Nihil Obstat:
Rt. Rev. Msgr. Victor R. Serrano, H.P.
Censor

Imprimatur:
Rt. Rev. Msgr. Benjamin L. Marino, P.A.
Vicar General - Chancellor
December 13, 1981

International Standard Book Number: 0-87793-229-8
(Cloth)
0-87793-230-1
(Paper)

Library of Congress Catalog Card Number: 81-67559

Cover and Text design: Elizabeth French

Darkness in the Marketplace

Contents

Preface

*T*he "marketplace" of our lives is where we live and love and where, to a large extent, we discover God. It is not, despite the title and tenor of the present book, all darkness. Even when the darkness predominates—in the various ways described in the pages which follow—still love is "the root and foundation" (Eph 3:17), not only in the love of the Lord but also in the love of all those he has given us to love. At times their love may not shed much light in our darkness, but even then it provides warmth. It sustains us and gives us life even on the darkest days.

I think of this now as I recall all my friends who have played a part in "warming" the writing of this book. Some of them are no longer alive: my father, Sister Stella Rosal (to whom *When the Well Runs Dry* was dedicated),[1] Nemrod Alfaro and Tony Izon, two of our San Jose seminarians who died during their seminary years. They, along with many other beloved friends living and dead, shared with me something of their own experience of the marketplace darkness about which we speak. They trusted me, shaped me, taught me how to write this book. They "warmed" me, as did others who played a more immediate part in the actual writing. The latter include three who

[1] Sister Stella died July 22, 1979—the feast of Mary Magdalene—the day before the first copies of the *Well* arrived in the Philippines.

typed the manuscript: Carol Crerar Green, my favorite sister-in-law; Segundiano Honorio, the ever-faithful secretary of San Jose Seminary; and one special member of the Sisters of Mercy of Rochester, New York, who has insisted on remaining anonymous despite my best efforts to persuade her otherwise. She seems to have taken Chapter 6 of the present book too much to heart! I can mention, however, her sister in religion, Sister Mary Bryan Ford, R.S.M., who is the parish assistant in Our Lady of Lourdes Parish in Rochester, and who used to check almost every morning after Mass on the progress of my writing. I wrote most of the manuscript during a four-month home visit in 1980 when the thought of facing Sister M.B. every morning had a wondrous effect on my perseverance!

As with the earlier books, I also owe much to my sister, Pidge James, and to Sister John Miriam Jones, S.C., to Gene Geissler and Ken Peters of Ave Maria Press, and to my Jesuit confreres, Fathers Charlie Wolf and Bill Abbott. Pidge and Sister John Miriam did much to provide a feminine (and occasionally feminist) perspective on the darkness in the marketplace. Father Bill made invaluable comments on several parts of the manuscript. All of them were more than generous with their encouragement.

I mentioned earlier that I have been warmed in the darkness of writing by all who have shared their lives and their inner journeys with me. They are true friends in the Lord, and this is really their book. I know that it will please them all that I dedicate it to one of their number—to my best friend, Marie Mooney Green, who also happens to be my mother.

Charged With the Grandeur of God

*T*he life of the mature Christian pray-er, and of the praying Christian community, is inevitably marked by the tension between contemplation and action, prayer and service. It has always been so and, judging from the gospel teaching of Jesus himself, it will always be so. He tells his beloved disciples, during his discourse at the Last Supper:

> If you belonged to the world,
> it would love you as its own;
> the reason it hates you
> is that you do not belong to the world.
> But I chose you out of the world (Jn 15:19).

Again, in his priestly prayer to his Father, he prays

> not for the world
> but for these you have given me,
> for they are really yours; (Jn 17:9)

and of these chosen ones he says:

9

They are not of the world,
any more than I belong to the world (Jn 17:16).

Yet these "anti-world" statements of the Lord are balanced, in the very same passages of St. John's Gospel, by a strong sense of mission to "the world," of life and service for the sanctification of this world:

I do not ask you (Father) to take them out of the world,
but to guard them from the evil one . . . .
As you have sent me into the world,
so I have sent them into the world,
I consecrate myself for their sakes now,
that they may be consecrated in truth (Jn 17:15, 18-19).

The disciples, like Jesus himself, are "in the world but not of the world." If this merely meant that the world was the irredeemable, hostile environment within which the disciples found themselves because of sin, and from which they had to escape by a yoga-like process of asceticism and withdrawal, the problem for Christian faith would not be so great. It would be difficult, of course, to live angelically in this sinful environment, but at least it would be perfectly clear who were the "good guys" and who the bad. As in the classic and simplistic Westerns of 30 or 40 years ago, one would always be able to tell the forces of good (the cowboys) from the forces of evil (the Indians). Everything, and everyone, would be black or white, with no shades of gray. The world would be unambiguously bad, and flight from it into the realm of pure contemplation of God would be clearly the only good. And, indeed, such a Christian vision of the world has attracted powerful support during the two thousand years of our history—from the Manichaean division between spirit (the work of the good God of Jesus) and flesh (created by, and subordinate to, an evil deity), through the Reformation stress on the radical sinfulness of man, to the recent tendency to divide the whole world into "godless" communists and God-fearing free men.[1] It is much easier for man, it would seem, to cope with a world in which good and evil are thus sharply distinguished—in which there is only black and white, with no confusing shades of gray to contend with.

For the biblical Christian, however, such a world does not exist. The first disciples, like us, wished it were so. But Jesus insisted they were wrong. In his vision, the evil weeds grow intermingled with the good wheat in this world of ours—so much so that we cannot totally uproot the weeds before the harvest without also destroying the wheat: St. Matthew recounts this striking parable of Jesus: "The reign of God may be likened to a man who sowed good seed in his field. While everyone was asleep, his enemy came and sowed weeds through his wheat, and then made off. When the crop began to mature and yield grain, the weeds made their appearance as well. The owner's slaves came to him and said, 'Sir, did you not sow good seed in your field? Where are the weeds coming from?' He answered, 'I see an enemy's hand in this.' His slaves said to him, 'Do you want us to go out and pull them up?' 'No,' he replied, 'pull up the

---

[1] Marxist-Leninist dogma, of course, tends to be equally simplistic, save that our angels are their devils, and vice-versa!

weeds and you might take the wheat along with them. Let them grow together until the harvest; then at harvest time I will order the harvesters, First collect the weeds and bundle them up to burn, then gather the wheat into my barn' " (Mt 13:24-30).

Somewhat later in the same chapter, Matthew has the disciples come to Jesus and say, "Explain to us the parable of the weeds in the field." And Jesus replies to them: "The farmer sowing good seed is the Son of Man; the field is the world, the good seed the citizens of the kingdom. The weeds are the followers of the evil one and the enemy who sowed them is the devil. The harvest is the end of the world, while the harvesters are the angels" (13:36-39). So this world of ours is a fertile field in which both good seed and evil, wheat and weeds, good men and bad, can flourish. And, mysteriously, both the weeds and the wheat must be allowed to grow together until the harvest time. Their roots are so intertwined in the same soil of the world—they grow so closely together—that a complete uprooting of the weeds would very likely also destroy the wheat. Moreover, I believe we can legitimately apply Jesus' parable to the individual Christian: That is, while Matthew has Jesus say that the field is the world, and the good and evil seed are good and evil men, I believe it is also true (particularly in the light of what St. Paul says, in Romans 7, about the "two laws" which are at war within every believer) that the field is the soul of the believer, and the good and evil seed are the good qualities and evil inclinations, the virtues and vices, which coexist in this little field. Here, too, it seems that the good and the evil must often be allowed to grow together until the harvest lest in totally uprooting the evil we also destroy the good.

Why is this so? I must admit that I cannot really understand it. Naturally speaking, it seems to me (as it does, I assume, to virtually every human being) that it would be better to destroy the weeds—that the field which is my soul is somehow polluted and unworthy of God because of their presence. But, at the same time, I have learned by experience that this complete eradication of the weeds is impossible to me, and equally impossible to those I direct. We must continually labor at the weeding of this garden of ours (whether the garden be the world or our own souls), and yet some weeds never seem to be eradicated.[2] So, while I do not really understand why the weeds must be allowed to grow with the wheat until the end, this passage (along with Romans 7) is one of the most consoling parts of Scripture for me. I suppose I don't need to know *why* the Lord is so tolerant, as long as I know *that* he is! The only response possible to me is to try to be as tolerant with myself and others as he is with us.

The world, then, is a mysterious, ambivalent reality for the biblical Christian: sometimes good, sometimes evil, sometimes the one soil in which both good and evil grow. The one thing that seems clear is

[2] We have discussed this mystery in another context in Chapter 2 ("The Water Is for the Flowers") of *When the Well Runs Dry*. There I distinguished between those failings which should be gradually eradicated if our prayer life is genuine, and those which may remain for a lifetime even in the dearest friends of God. St. John of the Cross makes a similar distinction, in discussing which "desires" block union with God and which do not.

that Christian faith (unlike some of the other great religions of history) cannot do without, or be understood apart from, the world. The incarnation of Jesus has forever committed God, for better or worse, to this world of ours. And where he is, his disciples must also be. They can be sanctified only where he was—in time and space and flesh. In the process they will experience all that he experienced—he who, "in the days when he was in the flesh, offered prayers and supplications with loud cries and tears to God, who was able to save him from death, and he was heard because of his reverence. Son though he was, he learned obedience from what he suffered" (Heb 5:7-8).

It is this world, mysterious and ambivalent and essential, which the present book is about. But we will look at the world, and the Christian's place in it, from a particular and limited perspective. For this book is intended as a sequel to *Opening to God* and *When the Well Runs Dry.*[3] It presupposes the vision of

---

[3] Ave Maria Press, Notre Dame, Indiana, 1977 and 1979 respectively. Because this book is a sequel to the earlier two, I shall refer frequently to points discussed in them. In doing so, I will try to summarize the argument referred to, so that the reader not familiar with *Opening to God* and *When the Well Runs Dry* may follow the discussion here even without reading the earlier books. Because the present discussion, however, of the relationship of prayer to the active life depends much on what we understand prayer to be, and on what we understand of the normal patterns of growth in souls committed to prayer, the new reader might find it helpful to read at least Chapter 1 and the Epilogue of *Opening to God,* as well as the Introduction ("To Tame and Be Tamed") of *When the Well Runs Dry.* In the latter I summarize the three stages of interior growth, the elaboration of which is the principal aim of *Opening* and the *Well.*

Christian prayer presented in those two books; and it
seeks to discover the relationship between the world
(the "marketplace" of our title), in which the pray-er
lives and serves, and the experience of mature prayer
which I have described as the "dry well," and which
Christian spirituality also knows as the "dark night"
or "the cloud of unknowing." Many questions, at
various levels, could be asked about the relationship
for the Christian between the marketplace and the
prie-dieu (the kneeler for prayer which is still com-
monly found in the sanctuaries of our churches), between active life in the world and Christian prayer.
The specific question to which the present book ad-
dresses itself is the following: What is the relationship
between prayer and service, between the "inner" and
the "outer" life, for one whose prayer has come to be
almost entirely dry and "passive"? In the *Well* (especially in Chapters 4 and 5), we described this experience of dryness or darkness, and explained its meaning and the way the committed pray-er should respond to it. We also (in Chapter 5, by means of the
image of "floating") attempted to show the goal of the
dry-well experience: what the Lord is leading us to,
by means of the dryness and darkness which runs so
counter to our own expectations and our own natural
desires. It was my hope that those who had come to
know the dry well as their own normal experience in
prayer would find in the *Well* some understanding of,
and thus the courage to accept, the mysterious and
painful way their beloved Lord was dealing with
them. Hundreds of letters I have received since the
Well appeared are blessed confirmation that my hope
has been fulfilled. Never, in fact, would I have

dreamed that the Lord was so deeply active in so many souls around the world.

As I reflected on these letters, however, and on my own experience as pray-er and as director, I realized that there was still more to be said about the dry well. Many souls, it seems, come to peace with the interior experience of dryness and darkness, and yet do not see the connection between this inner desert and their outer lives, their work in the world and their life in whatever communities the Lord has made them part of. Often there is a tension between the inner and the outer: work, family, community, social concern—all seem, somehow, to be obstacles to the contemplative work the Lord is bringing about in their souls. At times they feel that perhaps they are called to flee the world, to give themselves up totally, whether in a cloister or in a desert hermitage, to the work of interior transformation.[4] Or, if such flight is simply impossible (as it would be for the mother of a young family), they resign themselves to a split-level life, a sort of spiritual schizophrenia, in which the only relationship between their interior dry well and the demands of their active life in the world seems to be one of continual tension. Yet, the split and the tension need not exist. We hope to see that the outer and the inner—the marketplace and the prie-dieu, as I have characterized them in the chapters that

---

[4] I discussed this "temptation," and the way I myself experienced and resolved it, in Chapter 2 (pp. 64-67) of *When the Well Runs Dry*. In fact, in a sense this present book might be seen as an expansion and development of that chapter, in much the same way that the *Well* itself could be seen as an expansion of the Epilogue of *Opening to God*.

follow—are harmoniously integrated in the work of purification which we have called the dry well. It is the same God working, both at the prie-dieu and in the marketplace. The darkness in the marketplace of our active lives (in the "world") is as much a part of the dry-well experience of contemplation as is the inner darkness of our formal prayer. That, at least, is the conviction which led me to write this book.

When I began to reflect on this marketplace darkness, and to put my thoughts on paper, it was still not very clear to me *how* prie-dieu and marketplace were interrelated in the contemplative work. My "hero," St. John of the Cross, could not be of much direct help to me here,[5] since he writes for those who can, and are called to, withdraw totally from the marketplace. St. Teresa of Avila is much more helpful, since (I believe) she recognized that the marketplace—and thus the darkness in the marketplace—is as much a part of the cloistered, contemplative life as it is of life in the world. Her marketplace may be smaller than that of the active apostle or the lay Christian, but it is just as noisy and no less dark! But even Teresa did not experience, or directly discuss, the marketplace darkness as I, and most of my readers, are called to experience it.

On the other hand, while much has been written—especially since Vatican II—about the role of the Christian in the world, I do not believe that the contemplative dimension of this involvement has been much explored. There is a passage in a recent

---

[5] Although, as we shall see in Chapter 1, his *life* was very illuminating and instructive, even though his writings were not of great help with the present question.

book of Carlo Carretto which is very much to our point. The author, speaking to busy people who say they have no time to pray, writes, "Try to look at the reality in which you live—your work, your commitments, your relationships . . . —as a single whole from which you cannot disengage yourself, a whole which you have to think about. I shall say more: a whole by means of which God speaks to you and through which he guides you."[6] As Carretto's book makes clear, however, he is really concerned with a different question from ours. He is speaking to the urban man and woman of today, and he is seeking to show them how they can create, or discover, a desert (of contemplation) right in the midst of the city where they are called to live. By contrast, our concern is to discover how the "city" itself is really an integral part of the "divine desert" of contemplative transformation.

It would seem, then, that my readers and I are called to explore together what may be virgin territory. I have done so by asking first (in Part I) about the real link between the inner and the outer in the active-contemplative life. To my surprise (I have tried here, as in the first two books, to pray my way through the writing, with the result that I have often been quite surprised at what came out on paper!), St. Martha of Bethany became a central figure in this first part of the book. She has always figured in the Christian literature on prayer, but almost invariably as a foil for her sister, Mary, the true contemplative who had chosen "the better part." In my own reflections,

[6] Carlo Carretto, *The Desert in the City* (Collins, Cleveland and New York, 1979), p. 21.

Martha came to center stage: She taught me, as I hope she will teach my readers, some very beautiful lessons about the meaning of marketplace darkness (her kitchen being her marketplace) in the contemplative life of purification and transformation in God.

In Part II, I have tried to explore more deeply the three types of darkness in the marketplace which I discovered in Part I. When I began to write, the darkness I sought to explore was real but undifferentiated; many elements were mixed in together. As I proceeded, it became clear that this darkness was really *three* darknesses, each quite distinct and each playing a different role in what the author of *The Cloud of Unknowing* calls "the contemplative work." Moreover, as I sorted them out, the parallels between the interior darkness of the dry well and the outer darkness of the marketplace became clearer and clearer. It seemed evident that the Lord of love was really (as I suspected when I began) working to the same end in the marketplace and at the prie-dieu. This was an exciting discovery, because it meant that there is no need for spiritual schizophrenia in the life of the active contemplative. She really *is* "praying always"; he *is* a "contemplative in action" (to use the great Ignatian phrase) in a deeper sense than I had ever appreciated or realized before. I hope that, by God's grace, you will share some of my excitement, my sense of my life becoming "whole," as you read along with me.

In a sense, I already knew what I had discovered during these months of writing. This is why the title of the Epilogue is "To Arrive Where We Started," a line from T.S. Eliot's *Four Quartets* which I had occasion to quote already in the *Well* (page 150). The passage is one I loved long before I understood it (or do I really understand it even now?); similarly, I think I knew the meaning of the marketplace darkness long before I wrote this book, and yet only now do I "understand" it.

Perhaps I can explain better what I mean by referring to another poem which I have long loved. It is by Gerard Manley Hopkins, the greatest poet among my Jesuit brothers, and it captures perfectly the mystery of God's grandeur embodied in our darkness, so totally embodied that the two can not really be separated in Hopkins' vision:

> The world is charged with the grandeur of God.
>   It will flame out, like shining from shook foil;
>   It gathers to a greatness, like ooze of oil
> Crushed. Why do men then now not reck his rod?
> Generations have trod, have trod, have trod;
>   And all is seared with trade, bleared, smeared
>   with toil;
>   And wears man's smudge and shares man's smell;
>   the soil
> Is bare now, nor can foot feel, being shod.
>
> And for all this, nature is never spent;
>   There lives the dearest freshness deep down
>   things;
> And though the last lights off the black west went
>   Oh, morning, and the brown brink eastward,
>   springs—
> Because the Holy Ghost over the bent
>   World broods with warm breast and with ah!
>   bright wings.[7]

As I said, I have long loved Hopkins' poem; the mysterious interpenetration of wonder and sadness—wonder at the grandeur of God continually revealed in our world, and sadness that all is bleared, smeared, smudged in the hands of man, in my hands—has spoken to my experience for at least 30 years. It took much longer, though, to realize that the "grandeur" and the "smudging" were really fused together in the design of God, that he was and is, forever, Redeemer; that is, that, in taking on our sinful nature, he made sin his own. He *became* sin (incredible as it sounds) in order that we sinners might become holy. "For our sakes God made him who did not know sin, to be sin, so that in him we might become the very holiness of God" (2 Cor 5:21).

Did Hopkins realize this when he wrote "God's Grandeur"? Did he merely mean that the light of God and the darkness of man coexist side by side in this world of ours, with the Holy Spirit's light ultimately victorious? Or did he see more deeply, with St. Paul, that the Light and the darkness have interpenetrated so totally that the Light shines *in* the darkness and transforms the very darkness itself?

But then, who can *ever* really understand a God like this? I said earlier that I now understand the marketplace darkness of which I write. Yet, of course, I don't really understand it; that will take, quite literally, an eternity of exploration of the mys-

---

[7] Gerard Manley Hopkins, S.J., "God's Grandeur," from *The Poems of Gerard Manley Hopkins* (ed. W. H. Gardner and N. H. Mackenzie), 4th edition, Oxford University Press for the Society of Jesus, 1967.

terious depths of this beautiful God of ours. I can only hope that *Darkness in the Marketplace* will be, for me and for you who read it, one small step on that endless journey of discovery.

Part One

One

Darkness in Martha's Kitchen

*O*ne August Saturday, some 13 years ago, my father was sitting at the breakfast table looking out the kitchen window. When my mother entered the room, she saw his glum look and asked what was the matter. He replied: "Oh! It's raining and I can't cut the grass and do all the yard work that has to be done. The hedges beside the house need trimming. The shingles are coming off the garage roof. And besides, Pidge's wedding is soon and she'll be leaving us and will be all alone down there in Brooklyn!" As my mother quickly realized, his real trouble was losing his only daughter. But because of that, all the world looked black and every small problem seemed big even for one of the most optimistic and resilient men I have ever known.

All of us, I suspect, have had similar experiences. We know what a black mood is, or a dark day. And we know how easily some slight or frustration or anxiety can color our perception of everything around us. Even the sweetest mood can turn sour when someone close to us criticizes or misunderstands us. It has happened to all of us many times and, unless I miss my guess, it happened to a woman named Martha almost two thousand years ago. Martha of Bethany: sister of Mary and of Lazarus, friend of Jesus Christ, immortalized as one who "worried about many things" and missed the "one thing necessary." Poor Martha! We know so little about her, and yet she has become one of the most familiar figures of religious literature, her name somewhat unfairly made synonymous with the well-meaning but misguided worrywart and fuss-budget in so many of us.[1]

As I reflected about darkness—darkness in the marketplace—Martha came to dominate my thoughts. She seemed to capture beautifully, in the

---

[1] It is important to note that the symbolism which later Christian tradition has found in the figures of Mary and Martha goes far beyond the intentions of St. Luke or the content of their simple story in his gospel. Mary became a type of the contemplative life and Martha of the active—and they were often used to underscore the superiority of the contemplative life, although it is clear from St. Luke's whole gospel (which has been called the gospel of social concern) that the ideal disciple, for him, is one who combines the "pondering," listening, contemplative attitude of Mary with the generosity and fraternal service of Martha. My treatment of Martha in the pages that follow is consciously allegorical rather than exegetical. In this sense it is in the style of later Christian expansion on the text. But I believe that its content is more in the spirit of the whole Lucan vision of discipleship, in the sense that Christian service (action) and contemplation are seen as complementary, and not as mutually exclusive. That is why I would say that the authentic disciple of Jesus, even in a cloistered community, really has a hyphenated name: "Mary-Martha"!

one little incident which has made her immortal—or rather in what must have happened after that incident, though Scripture is silent about the sequel— what this book is really all about. I came to see Martha with new eyes, to love her in a way I had not before now. She "came alive" for me.

But let me not get ahead of my story. As I noted in the Introduction, this book is basically a sequel to *When the Well Runs Dry,* in which I explored that experience of prayer "beyond the beginnings" which has been variously called a "dark night," a "cloud of unknowing," a "prayer of faith." For a long time I have felt that this dry-well experience would have a special quality in the life of someone called to the active, apostolic life. It is true, as I stressed in Part 2 of the *Well,* that the inner experience of darkness is, when it comes, essentially the same for a cloistered nun or a mother of a young family. I believe it is very difficult, however, for active people to see the connection between this inner experience (even when they do come to accept it and be at peace in the darkness) and what is happening in their outer lives of work and family. Even the deepest pray-er (and perhaps especially such a person) can feel as if he or she is living a divided life.

Yet how is the inner experience of the dark night (or dry well) integrated into a life of active involvement in the world and of apostolic service? The feeling I had as I began to reflect on that question is that, for "apostles," the process of purification and taming whereby we become "floaters" in the Lord (i.e., whereby we learn to let go of our own efforts to love and serve the Lord according to our own ideas of what is best, and to let him take control of our lives)[2] is accomplished not only in formal prayer but in all the events of our active lives. I felt that, because most mature pray-ers fail to realize this, their lives become split. The frustrations and trials and challenges of their outer lives are seen as a distraction from, or an obstacle to, the inner experience of God which has become more and more the center of their lives and desires.

This somewhat negative view of the active side of our lives—the idea that active involvement is somehow an obstacle to inner depth—is not *entirely* false. It does capture a real dimension of our experience, one that led St. Ignatius Loyola to state that his Jesuits should be "in the world but not of the world"; one that led St. Paul to exclaim that he gladly counted everything else as "rubbish" compared to the ineffable knowledge and possession of Jesus Christ (Phil 3:8). Strong words, indeed! And they are echoed in the "nada" doctrine of St. John of the Cross: Everything but God himself is nothing ("nada") for one who has truly begun to experience the overwhelming power of his love. Thus all other attachments which compete with God in our hearts must be broken, uprooted.

There is then a very clear tradition of conflict between the inner experience of Jesus Christ and all the beauties and attachments of this created world of ours. It is a tradition which retains its value even in a

---

[2] See Chapter 6 of *When the Well Runs Dry* for a fuller discussion of this contrast between the floater and the swimmer in the sea of the Lord. The same contrast is discussed, in its apostolic dimension in Chapter 2 of the present book.

strongly incarnational age such as ours. There comes a point in every mature pray-er's life where God wishes to encounter the soul *directly,* and where all creatures, all efforts, even words seem to be obstacles to that encounter. The words of St. John of the Cross, "From today do not send me other messengers, for they cannot tell me what I need to hear,"[3] become painfully meaningful at that time. The mature pray-er knows then experientially what Paul means in describing all that is not Jesus Christ as "rubbish." Yet, while Paul longed to be dissolved and to be with Christ, he chose instead to remain "for your sakes" (Phil 1:21-26). Somehow his own desire to be with the Lord was to be fulfilled precisely by this remaining behind. St. Ignatius also illustrates this paradox when he speaks of the world as merely a "means" to God, from which we must be wholly detached,[4] and yet he also sees the world as the field of service in which the "contemplative in action" is to seek and find God in all things. In the writings of St. John of the Cross the problem is approached differently, perhaps because he writes from the perspective of a "contemplative" for whom the renunciation of all things for God is the central thrust. That is, the apparent tension between absorption in Christ and life "in the world" may not be evident in John's

[3] *The Spiritual Canticle,* stanza 6. The "messengers," as John tells us, are the knowledge and feelings we have of him through the mediation of creation and by the use of our natural faculties.

[4] See, for example, the famous prayer of Ignatius which begins "Take and receive, O Lord, all my liberty. Take my memory, my understanding, my will . . ." The radical character of the gift has made many retreatants, over the past 400 years, very uncomfortable about making this prayer their own!

writing, since the apostolic concern is not explicit or central for him.[5] The problem of integrating the active life into a mature spirituality is not at first seen as a real problem by John's reader, since the "active life" seems to play a very slight part in his vision. It is striking, for example, that a recent index for the writings of St. John of the Cross[6] does not include any entries at all for the words "apostolate," "ministry," "service." And John's writings provide only one reference to St. Martha, namely, the introduction to Stanza 29 of the *Spiritual Canticle*. There John has this to say: "(The) soul, indeed lost to all things and won over to love, no longer occupies her spirit in anything else. She even withdraws in matters pertinent to the active life and exterior occupations for the sake of fulfilling the one thing the bridegroom said was necessary (Lk 10:42), and that is: attentiveness to God and continual love of him. This the Lord values and esteems so highly that he reproved Martha when she tried to call Mary away from her place at his feet in order to busy her with other active things in his service; and Martha thought that she herself was doing all the work and that Mary, because she was enjoying the Lord's presence, was doing nothing (Lk

[5] This apostolic concern is, in fact, much more prominent in the writings of St. Teresa of Avila than in John's. For this reason I have suspected that Teresa, if she lived today, might well be a "contemplative in action"—perhaps a Carmelite missionary. In her day and place, religious life for women was inevitably a cloistered life. Thus she never faced the choice between apostolate and cloister which John consciously made.

[6] Compiled by the sisters of the Bronx, New York, Carmel (1978), to supplement the recent English translation by Kavanaugh and Rodriguez (Washington, D.C., 1973).

10:39-41). Yet, since there is no greater nor more necessary work than love, *the contrary is true.*"[7] This last phrase, which I have italicized, implies that it was really *Martha* who was doing nothing![8] Yet, even in John of the Cross's *life* (as distinct from his writings), the problem and the link we seek clearly emerge. He was imprisoned by his former brethren in the Calced Carmelites, confined to a small cell and scourged several times a week in an effort to persuade him to retract his "errors" and confess his fault. This outer darkness provided the climate in which John began the composition of his great work on the inner darkness of the soul. Even after his release, when the storms of conflict subsided somewhat and he was able to complete his great mystical writings, John was called to lead a very busy and intensely active life: as prior of various monasteries, as a member of the governing board of the Discalced Carmelites and as Vicar-Provincial of Andalusia in Southern Spain. Finally, as his short life drew to a close, he was caught in the painful struggle within the Carmelite reform over the direction which that reform should take. In the short term, John was on the losing side in this fraternal strife. He lost his positions in the Carmelite government, and there was even a move afoot—cut short

[7] Page 523 in the translation of Rodriguez and Kavanaugh.

[8] As I noted above, St. Teresa presents a much more positive picture of the active life, and of the complementarity of the two lives in the church. See, for example, Chapter 3 of *The Way of Perfection* (pp. 46-47 in the Doubleday-Image edition of E. Allison Peers' translation). And for a beautiful discussion of how Martha and Mary must "work together," see *The Way of Perfection,* Chapter 17 (Peers, pp. 126-127); and "working together" even in one person, Chapter 31 (Peers, p. 203).

by his early death at 49 in 1591—to expel him from the new order to which he had given his whole priestly life.[9]

In the providence of God, this pattern of intrigue and frustration and misunderstanding is not at all uncommon in the lives of the saints. Indeed, it would seem to be the usual pattern. The striking fact is that John of the Cross, despite his doctrine of "nada" and withdrawal, experienced so fully not only the intense activity but also the darkness of the marketplace, of the "outer" world. The point I wish to make here is that I believe this paradox is not really so surprising when viewed from the divine perspective. That is why I consider John's life, given his writing and his emphasis on withdrawal, the most striking instance of the link between the dark night and the marketplace. I suspect that the mystery I am exploring in this book is most clearly exemplified in John's own experience, once we realize that the "nada" (the detachment it implies) is *not* the end of the spiritual journey, nor even the end of the earthly phase of that journey. Once I am truly free, truly detached in the proper sense of that word,[10] what

[9] There is a very good short summary of John's life and times in the General Introduction (pp. 16-33) of Kavanaugh and Rodriguez's edition of *The Collected Works of St. John of the Cross* (Institute of Carmelite Studies, Washington, D.C., 1973).

[10] "Free from" all else in order, and only in order, that I might be totally "free for" God. It is this sense which binds St. Ignatius Loyola and St. John of the Cross closely together. Unless we thereby become free *for* one great love, our efforts to be free *from* other attachments would lead only to a dehumanized, anti-incarnational state of apathy—and not to real holiness. See John's *Ascent of Mount Carmel*, Book 1, Chapter 11 (p. 97 in Kavanaugh and Rodriguez), where John uses the beautiful

then? Normally I do not die physically. Nor do I cease to be touched by the challenges and the needs of the world in which I am rooted. So here we find sharply focused the question which confronted me as I set about writing this book: Once I have truly and freely surrendered to God, truly said "yes" to his being the God of my life, what part does this world and my involvement in it play in the work of God in me? Is it an essential part? Is it so for *every* mature Christian pray-er, whatever his or her particular calling may be? "Detachment" is so widely identified even by committed Christians and pray-ers with non-concern and non-involvement that it may be surprising to the reader that I even suggest the possibility that one *can* be, and that God might desire one to be, *both* detached and truly involved. I am not sure that John of the Cross would have been comfortable with this possibility,[11] although I do believe it was abundantly embodied in his own life and in his lived experience of God.

To return, then, to our question, what is the value of our life "in the world" once we have freely surrendered to God—once the soul has begun to

---

image of a bird who cannot fly until all the ropes and threads, which tie her to earth, have been cut. St. Paul expresses a similar idea in Romans 6:22.

[11] For a very strong statement in favor of non-involvement, of total withdrawal, see *The Spiritual Canticle,* Stanza 29, paragraphs 2 and 3 (Kavanaugh and Rodriguez, pp. 523-524), which follows immediately after the reference to Martha quoted above. Cf., though, his brief comments in *The Spiritual Canticle,* (Stanza 36, especially paragraphs 4, 11-12) and *The Dark Night* (Book 2, Chapter 19, #3) on the value of creation *after* we are truly united to God.

experience the deeper, drier reaches of prayer? As I have implied above, and as I hope to show in the chapters that follow, I believe this life "in the world" plays an essential, integral part in our inner growth toward divine union. The point is made beautifully, in allegorical fashion, by Hannah Hurnard. In *Mountains of Spices,* she has Much Afraid, the heroine of *Hinds Feet on High Places* (the story of Much Afraid's withdrawal to the mountain of God), return from the mountain to her home Valley of Humiliation. She returns, transformed into Grace and Glory, to share with all her Fearing relatives what she herself has experienced.[12] Moreover, she does not merely share the riches of the mountains; she is resented, envied, resisted—and loved, praised and followed. All of these experiences form part of the way the Lord continues in her the work he began on the mountain. Grace and Glory's return to the valley is not only for the sake of others. She needs it too: The valley (the marketplace) is where the good work begun in her is to be brought to perfection.

That this is so seems abundantly clear from Jesus' own life and from his teaching on the apostolate and on the place of the cross in the disciple's life. It is also clear from Paul's reflections on the apostolic calling as he experienced it himself.[13] In fact, it seems to me

[12] Cf. Mary Magdalene in John 20:17: "Do not cling to me, Mary . . . but go to my brethren and tell them . . ."

[13] See 1 Corinthians, chapters 1 to 4 and 2 Corinthians, chapters 1 to 7. The letters of Paul to Corinth are a particularly valuable source for our reflections on darkness in the marketplace. Paul encountered much misunderstanding, criticism and even persecution in his attempt to form the church of Corinth according to the Spirit of Jesus Christ. And this forced him to some

that the whole of the New Testament makes one thing abundantly clear: Allowing always for the *special* (and very beautiful) call of Mary to forget everything else and simply to sit at the feet of the Lord and be absorbed in him,[14] it is *usually* his will that we be able to keep him only by giving him away.

In the incident at Bethany, when Jesus visited Mary and Martha and Lazarus, Martha complained to Jesus, "Lord, are you not concerned that my sister has left me to do the household tasks all alone? Tell her to help me." The Lord answered, "Martha, Martha, you are anxious and upset about many things; one thing only is required. Mary has chosen the better portion[15] and she shall not be deprived of it" (Lk 10:40-42). Mary's is the *better* way, because it is the way of eternity, of heaven. But, I believe, Martha's is the *usual* way while we are on the journey toward heaven. I would even say Martha's is the better way if we evaluate it in relation to our present situation as wayfarers. Why? Because of the important part that our involvement and service, and the "darkness" it necessarily brings, plays in our own process of

---

soul-searching reflection on the link between his apostolic ministry and his personal love for Jesus Christ. The chapters noted are a treasure for every frustrated apostle in succeeding ages.

[14] As I hope will be clear from the chapters that follow, and as many cloistered contemplatives have made clear to me in sharing their lives, the "darkness in the marketplace" is also an essential part of the cloistered vocation even though the marketplace in question may be only the size of their small, enclosed monastery.

[15] Literally, "Mary has chosen the good portion." Note that it is St. John (chapter 11) who identifies Mary and Martha as the sisters of Lazarus, and who says their home was in Bethany.

transformation. I hope we can see in the present book why (in the view of Scripture) Martha's way is normally and necessarily the way of the wayfarer en route to transformation in God.

Scripture catches St. Martha at one moment in her life with the Lord—one frustrating moment for her. When Grace and Glory returns from the High Places to the Valley of Humiliation, her attempts to share what she has discovered are often marked by obscurity, frustration, failure and misunderstanding. Similarly, Martha's efforts to please the Lord lead to frustration and gentle rebuke. What is the relation between this moment of darkness and her own love for Jesus? Was she simply "wrong" in her reaction, or is this experience a very important part of her own inner journey, where the Lord was working his will in her just as much as he was in Mary sitting at his feet? That is, is Martha simply mistaken, or is her "mistake" an essential part of her growth? St. Luke does not tell us, of course, and there is no scriptural evidence to guide us in discovering the actual effect of this incident in Martha's life. But, since most of us can find *ourselves* very easily in the person and reaction of Martha here, I think it is fruitful to let our imaginations explore the sequel to the gospel incident. We do this not to write a fanciful history of Martha but rather to understand more concretely the "Martha" in each of us. In this spirit, then, I think we can say of Martha that, given her character and her mood at the time, there must have been real "darkness in the kitchen" when she returned there after the Lord's rebuke! After all, she really loved him. In fact, it is precisely her love that gives the sting to his reply.

She must have wondered if all her efforts to love and serve him were misguided. Does he mean that she too should just sit at his feet and let everyone starve? Maybe we have focused too much on Mary in this gospel story. What is happening in that suddenly dark kitchen may be of even more importance for our own inner lives. Let us follow Martha back to the kitchen, to see what we can learn. If we are fortunate, the Lord may follow too, to speak to her troubled heart—and to ours. That is the grace we seek, for it is "Martha called to contemplation" for whom this book is written.[16]

[16] Martha has often received attention in the great writings on prayer. The author of *The Cloud of Unknowing,* for example, devotes several brief chapters to the Martha and Mary symbolism. St. Teresa of Avila, in Chapter 17 of *The Way of Perfection,* uses Martha as a symbol of the active life, of those *not* called to contemplation and yet called to be made perfect in another way. There is, however, a revealing passage in this chapter (p. 127 in the Peers translation, Doubleday Image, 1964) which strongly implies that, for Teresa, even Martha is called to "contemplation" (i.e., the passive or receptive prayer of the dry well or dark night): "I do not mean that it is for us to say what we shall do, but that we must do our best in everything (i.e., as she says just before this, "contemplation and mental and vocal prayer and tending the sick and serving in the house and working at even the lowliest tasks"), for the choice is not ours but the Lord's . . . for he is wise and powerful and knows what is fitting for you and for himself as well. Be sure that, if you do what lies within your power and prepare yourself for high contemplation with the perfection aforementioned, then, if he does not grant it to you—*and I think he will not fail to do so if you have true detachment and humility*—it will be because he has laid up this joy for you . . . in heaven." Thus Teresa allows for the possibility that there may be another "active" way to reach true holiness; but the phrase I have italicized makes clear, I believe, that she felt that, in the Lord's actual plan for us, even Martha is called to contemplation. I have expressed the same opinion in *When the Well Runs Dry,* pp. 161 ff.

Two

Working for God *vs.* Doing God's Work

*M*artha's dark thoughts probably represent the painful starting point of the contemplative phase of every contemplative-active vocation. We are converted from a life centered on self to a life centered in the Lord; we realize that this life, like Jesus' own, must be "for others," lived in service; and we eagerly set about being men and women for others, committed to changing the world for Christ, making all things new in him. And then he "rebukes" us, tells us that our zeal is misplaced, that some apparently idle friend or neighbor has really "chosen the better portion." The rebuke is painful precisely because we, like Martha, were doing it "all for him." We find ourselves asking: What *do* you want? Have I really been mistaken in my zeal for you? Were my efforts to love and serve you all illusion?

Before we pursue this crucial line of questioning, though, one important point must be noted: Martha was lucky in that it was clearly *the Lord* who was rebuking her, i.e., she knew it was *he* complaining, and she had to face that fact, painful as it might be. Very often we don't recognize that it is the Lord himself frustrating our efforts—we don't hear his voice in the "rebuke," but the voice of other persons: narrow-minded, censorious, blind to the needs we ourselves see, lacking in the zeal we ourselves have for the Lord's work. There are dark thoughts in our kitchen, but they are directed not versus the Lord but versus "Lazarus" and "Mary." Those who disagree with, and block, our vision of what needs to be done are seen as frustrating the *Lord's* work! Our activity, we feel, is correctly conceived and necessary, but other people (and the devil!) are the obstacles. And so, we think, the Martha story does not really apply to us at all; more applicable to our situation is Jesus' confrontation with the Pharisees in John 5, 7 and 8. It is "God and I" against the forces of evil, and God is as frustrated with them as I am!

But is this really true? Since very few of us are ever going to hear the Lord's correcting voice directly (even Teresa of Avila, who was on rare, familiar terms with him, usually received her corrections through confessors, inquisitors and other fallible human instruments), how do we decide whether God is speaking to us—even "rebuking" us—through the opposition and criticism of others, or whether they are really working against God in opposing us?

The question is clearly one of *discernment* (the place where prayer meets action), and can be answered only by a truly discerning heart. This means that we cannot decide correctly whether it is the Lord or the devil that is frustrating our efforts, through the human opposition and criticism we meet, unless and until we bring the frustration to prayer. Once we do, it is a cardinal principle of discernment that the Lord always speaks in peace. Even if he is rebuking or chastizing those he loves, there will always be peace if the rebuke is truly his voice. It might help in clarifying this point to note what St. Teresa says about genuine humility (*The Way of Perfection,* Chapter 39, Peers, p. 257): "Pay great attention, daughters, to this point which I shall now make, because sometimes thinking yourself so wicked may be humility and virtue and at other times a very great temptation . . . . Humility, however deep it be, neither disquiets nor troubles nor disturbs the soul; it is accompanied by peace, joy and tranquillity. Although, on realizing how wicked we are, we can see clearly that we deserve to be in hell . . . , yet, if our humility is true, this distress is accompanied by an interior peace and joy of which we should not like to be deprived. Far from disturbing or depressing the soul, it enlarges it and makes it fit to serve God better. The other kind of distress only disturbs and upsets the mind and troubles the soul . . . . I think the devil is anxious for us to believe that we are humble and, if he can, to lead us to distrust God." In *The Way,* Chapter 41 (especially pp. 268-271) she makes a similar distinction in discussing "fear of the Lord": The holy fear which is a sure sign of virtue is freeing, produces confidence and courage; it is far from the counterfeit fear which makes us timorous, hesitant to risk, even scrupulous, and which is the work of the devil. The paradox in this description of holy fear is resolved on page 270: "For we are weak and we cannot trust ourselves, and the more determined we are, the less *self*-confidence we should have, for confidence must come *from God*. But when we find ourselves in this state, we need not feel constrained or depressed, for the Lord will help us . . . ." And if we feel that the devil and the world are blocking our efforts to serve the Lord, this feeling, too, must always be marked by peace (and charity and humility and detachment),[1] if we are to trust it as a sure sign of God's view of the situation.

This may sound very good in theory, but how difficult it is in practice! How easily we identify our reactions and perceptions with the Lord's—and then are filled with anger and frustration and righteous indignation (rather than charity and detachment and humility) that *his* designs are blocked by the forces of evil. And as long as we try to settle the question at the level of reason and natural feeling, the indignation is inevitable and inescapable for zealous and dedicated souls. The situations of injustice we face, whether personal or social, will be such as to virtually compel an agitated (rather than a peaceful) response, and the devil will be working overtime to convince us this anxious sense of urgency *must* be the right course. "What need is there to waste time discerning, when the evil, and its cause, is so obvious?" If we reply, as we should, that it is not "the evil and its cause" which we wish to discern, but rather the way *the Lord is*

---

[1] These are the three crucial foundation stones of any genuine contemplative life, to which St. Teresa devotes Chapters 1 to 15 of *The Way of Perfection*.

reacting to this evil and *wants us to react* to it,[2] then the voice (God's? the devil's?) replies: "But that is clear already! From Scripture. From the church's teachings. From the evident signs of the times. What need is there to discern when God's will is obvious?"

The argument is very subtle (though it appears quite straightforward)—and very dangerous. Once we find ourselves thinking there is no need to discern—no need to test our conclusions and convictions and especially our inspirations to act—I feel we can be sure it is *not* the Lord speaking to us. As Paul says: "Our battle is not against human forces but against the principalities and powers, the rulers of this

[2] This distinction, which may not be so obvious at first sight, is really crucial. Discernment is related to *action:* It involves a judgment about (and a commitment to) the *action* desired *by the Lord* in a concrete situation, and not merely a judgment about the rightness or wrongness of the situation itself. The two are closely related, of course, and normally the latter (intellectual) judgment is *one* basis for the former (volitional) commitment to a course of action. That is, very simply, "This is right and that is wrong" is *a* basis for the committed judgment, "I will do this and not that." The various types of situational analysis (whether Marxist or structuralist, or post-Marxist or post-structuralist) which are widely used today are, I believe, ways to make that very important intellectual judgment about the rightness or wrongness of human social situations. But I stressed that this intellectual judgment is only *"one* basis," *a* basis for the volitional commitment which discernment is immediately concerned with. The mind's judgment about right and wrong is not decisive by itself in determining how we should respond (and this is perhaps the major flaw in much current stress on situational analysis): There is no doubt, it seems to me, that Calvary was "wrong," the work of evil men in a corrupt institutional situation and yet Jesus discerned that it was the Father's will for him that he submit "like a lamb led to the slaughter." No amount of structural analysis could ever have led the Lord to this commitment to act, to respond in this way!

world of darkness, the evil spirits in regions above. You must put on the armor of God if you are to resist on the evil day; do all that your duty requires, and hold your ground" (Eph 6:12-13).

And in this warfare, not with flesh and blood men only but with principalities and powers, it is a further cardinal principle of discernment that the devil always seeks to enter as an angel of light[3]—that is, he always tempts us in ways that appear good and reasonable to us. And for people who have learned to love the Lord, this will mean that the devil must counterfeit the voice of God in order to lead them astray.

In the situation which was the springboard for this discussion—where a person seeking to serve the Lord, like Martha, encounters frustration and opposition and, perhaps, rebuke—the devil's most effective line of attack will be to convince the troubled soul that those opposing him are opposing God, that it is clear what God wants, and that there is no need to discern. But we must note that not every discernment situation in our lives, thank God, is one of frustration and opposition; the devil can, and will, be just as active when all is "smooth sailing," when success and the approval of others seem to guarantee that our work is God's will. This latter situation is, in fact, perhaps more dangerous than the "darkness in the kitchen" from which we began.

---

[3] The expression is from Paul's Second Letter to the Corinthians (11:14) and is quoted in the rules of St. Ignatius Loyola for discernment (*Spiritual Exercises,* Rules for Discernment for the Second Week, rule #4). It is also found in St. Teresa, *The Way of Perfection,* Chapter 38 (Peers, p. 249).

We are concerned in this book with the darkness, the frustration, the lack of success in the life of the contemplative in action which, inevitably, will overflow from the dry well of prayer to the busy marketplace of action. But it is good to note that even in good times (whether in prayer or in apostolic service) we must be cautious and discerning. Not every consolation, not every apostolic success, is from the Lord. They, too, must be tested by their fruits: humility, detachment, charity (even for our "enemies") and, coloring them all, peace. The devil is willing to join the Tridentine choir and sing Gregorian chant in praise of God, if thereby he can bring the soul to his chosen end!

Some people have a martyr complex, and become more stubbornly self-righteous the more they are frustrated and challenged. But most of us take the Lord for granted in good times and are only brought to our knees in hard times. Thus it is usually only when things are dark that we, like Martha, begin to suspect that the Lord may not see things as we do. This is a very painful experience, as it surely was for Martha; and yet, once we have lived through it and discovered the lesson the Lord is teaching, we will come to count this suffering as one of the great graces of our lives. We will realize how shallow was our security when all our efforts to love and serve the Lord seemed to be blessed by success. Or, conversely, we will begin to realize how mistaken we were in envying the apostolic success of others and in taking it as a sign that they were closer to the Lord, giving more pleasing service to him.

The preceding paragraph expresses, as best I can,

one of the deepest and most precious lessons of my
own life. And it forms the leitmotiv, the dominant
theme, of this whole book. When St. Paul says that
"God's folly is wiser than men, and his weakness
more powerful than men," he is referring to the message of Calvary, of victory through failure, which was
at the very heart of his ministry and preaching: "The
message of the cross is complete absurdity to those
who are headed for ruin, but to us who are experienc-
ing salvation it is the power of God . . . . Has not
God turned the wisdom of this world into folly? Since
in God's wisdom the world did not come to know him
through 'wisdom,' it pleased God to save those who
believe through the absurdity of the preaching of the
gospel. Yes, Jews demand 'signs' and Greeks look for
'wisdom,' but we preach Christ crucified—a stum-
bling block to Jews, and an absurdity to Gentiles; but
to those who are called, Jews and Greeks alike, Christ
the power of God and the wisdom of God. For God's
folly is wiser than men, and his weakness more powerful than men" (1 Cor 1:18-25). This beautiful passage itself can serve as a test of the depth of our
experience: If we find Paul's words deeply moving, it
can only be because we have ourselves experienced
something of the paradox of God's ways, and of the
transcendent value of "failure" in bringing us to him.
On the other hand, if the passage strikes us merely as
a rather convoluted play on words, then I suspect we
have not yet begun to discover in our own lives the
paradoxical truth that Paul is struggling to express—a
truth which all of us, naturally speaking and at the
beginning of our conversion, find a scandal and a
folly. We are all "Jews" and "Greeks" when first we

are brought face to face with the full reality of Calvary in our lives.

The remaining chapters will, I hope, spell out in concrete detail the specific ways our good God accomplishes this revolutionary inversion of values in the lives of those who are called not merely to pray at the dry well of contemplation but to work in the dark marketplace of his world. It can be seen already, from our discussion of Martha and her dark-kitchen mood, that there is, for the contemplative apostle, a real parallel in their experience of prayer and action. The whole prayer experience of the dry well, the dark night, the cloud of unknowing, represents a complete shift in perspective for the apostle, whether that "apostle" be called to raise a family or run a parish or govern a country. In both prayer and action this shift in perspective, this inversion of values, will be painful and disorienting.

Speaking of prayer, John of the Cross says that many reach this point of inversion,[4] but few pass beyond it. For contemplatives in action, I believe, the same is true, and for the same reasons: fear to trust the Lord as he leads into "the foolishness of God"; lack of good spiritual direction; and excessive reliance on our natural ways of interpreting and judging the "dark marketplace" situations of our lives.

For several years I have been teaching a course in "Apostolic Prayer," attempting to explore the link between prayer and action in the life of the committed pray-er in the world. The best way I have found to

---

[4] It corresponds to Book One of his *Dark Night of the Soul* (the "night of the senses") and also to Chapter 4 ("The Potter's Clay") of *When the Well Runs Dry*.

explain this critical moment in the life of the active pray-er is to distinguish between "working for God" and "doing God's work." At first sight, the two phrases appear equivalent but there is a crucial difference between them. Let me try to clarify it by the use of a homely example, which has proven quite effective in my course.

Suppose Christmas is approaching, and a friend wishes to give me a gift. There are two ways she can go about it. She can, first, try to decide what I would like—and what she would like to give me—and then shop for the gift of her choice. Or, she can ask me what I would like and then give me what I request, provided she can afford it. Suppose she does it the second way; and suppose when she asks me what I would most like, I say "blue cheese." Since I am known in my family as a blue cheese addict, and since blue cheese is rare in the Philippines, the example is not at all fanciful. But for my Filipino friend it does present some problems: Blue cheese is scarce, it has a "fragrance" which Filipinos find repugnant, and those who have tried it generally don't like it! So my friend might well reply, "Ugh! blue cheese! I could never give that to *anyone* as a gift!" So she finds herself with a problem: She knows that I would like, but she has no desire to give it to me. What will she do? It all depends on whether she really wants to give me a gift of *her* choice or to give me whatever *I* would like, however repugnant it might be to her.[5]

_____

[5] The first time I used this example in class, I had a blue cheese fiesta the following Christmas! And when a group of the seminarians told me of their experience—in locating a store that sold it, in facing down the puzzled stares and offended

I suspect the application to our life with God is already clear. We can "work for him"; that is, we can choose what we want to give him, what we want him to like, what we think he needs and desires. Or we can ask him what he would like and do whatever he wishes—"do his work"—no matter how repugnant it may be to us. The latter is much more costly, since we may find that he too likes the "blue cheese" which repels us. But it is the only way of being sure to please him. If, instead, we choose the gift ourselves—if we decide what we want to give him and what we think he really needs and should want—he will surely be grateful for and pleased by the love symbolized by our gift. But it may not be what he really wants and can really use. And, as we shall see, if we are lucky we will become frustrated with our chosen way!

Which way do most people give gifts? In our human friendships it seems clear enough. We have closets or cabinets filled with gifts received—gratefully received but unwanted and unneeded—which we in turn can give to someone else (provided only it not be to the original giver!) the next time Christmas comes around.[6] Similarly, one who "works for God" chooses what he believes God does, or should, want—what he wants the Lord to want. St. Ignatius Loyola believed that this is not at all rare; in

---

noses of the other customers and the pedestrians on the street (blue cheese has a uniquely wonderful pungency and sliminess in the tropic heat!)—I realized how apt my example is!

[6] Of course, if the giver is very dear to us we may have to ignore our own desires, and wear, or display, the gift—at least when the giver is present! And we may even come to love the gift simply *because* it comes from one we love.

the *Spiritual Exercises,* when discussing the way to make a good and holy choice (an "election"), he says, "Many first choose marriage, which is a means, and secondarily to serve God our Lord in the married state, which service of God is the end." In Ignatius' more academic terminology, they choose the *means* (e.g., marriage) first and then seek to employ the means chosen to achieve their *end* (the love and service of God). But, Ignatius tells us, this is not really the proper way to proceed. We should first choose our end, our goal, and then choose (or reject) the various possible means only insofar as they help us to achieve our goal.

When it comes to God, which way do most of us usually act? In my courses on prayer and discernment, there are usually a number of married students. When I cite and explain Ignatius' example, the expressions on their faces seem to reflect a distinct uneasiness, an inner realization that they (good and prayerful people) had really chosen the means (marriage) first, and were now seeking to employ that means to realize the end of their lives, the love and service of God. I have never wanted to embarrass them by asking them pointblank what they were thinking. But, from my own experience of the choices I have made and the choices my directees have shared with me,[7] I feel quite sure I know. It is a mark of a rare spiritual maturity to subordinate all our

[7] Priesthood, like marriage, is also a "means" in Ignatius' sense. Hence, it must be chosen in subordination to the "end," which is, as always, the love and service of the Lord. This means discovering that it is really the means whereby he wishes me to accomplish the end of love and service.

choices to the end we seek; and that maturity, it would seem, is only achieved by a long schooling in the dark night of prayer. The dark night or the dry well is precisely, from an apostolic point of view, the Lord's way of freeing us from all those "inordinate attachments" which prevent us from being single-hearted and single-minded in our choices and which keep us from subordinating every "means" to the end of the praise and glory of God.[8]

It may seem that we have wandered far from the

---

[8] It is here that I see the deep affinity and the complementarity of St. Ignatius and St. John of the Cross. The *Spiritual Exercises* of Ignatius are an inspired tool for *beginning* the process of achieving freedom from our inordinate attachments—our attachments to means without proper subordination to our end. But they are "exercises"; the stress is on our own effort (aided, of course, by grace). And this effort *alone,* as John of the Cross has made abundantly clear (and this is the teaching which has made him a Doctor of the church), cannot carry us very far. The *active* purification of the soul is, as John affirms, the essential first step to holiness, but the process of purification can never be completed by our ascetical and meditative exercises alone. It is a process of divinization (cf., I Jn 3:1-3), and only the Lord's direct and all-consuming action can effect our divinization. St. Ignatius realized this, of course, and captured it implicitly in the magnificent vision of the "third degree of humility," and in the grace of confirmation which is the goal of the third and fourth weeks of the *Exercises.* Moreover, at every point of the *Spiritual Exercises,* the (sometimes very detailed) activity which Ignatius prescribes is always ordered to the *grace* (e.g., of sorrow for sin, of personal knowledge of Jesus) which the retreatant seeks as a free gift of God. But just as John, given his charism and temperament, can easily be misread as negative and "anti-world," so too Ignatius can easily be misread as "activist" and semi-Pelagian. Neither of them is well-served by "disciples" too narrow-minded or too unimaginative to recognize the complementarity of their visions—an inevitable complementarity, since it is the same Lord of love whom both of them encountered in such extraordinary depth.

darkness in Martha's kitchen. But I don't think so. What we have discovered is that the first meaning of that darkness is probably that Martha (as we have imagined her, a concrete symbol for the "Martha-in-us") has reached a critical point in her relationship to the Lord she loves. Until now, she has been "working for God": Her busyness with the cooking and cleaning and setting the table was all done out of love for him. It was what she thought he would like, what she wanted to give him. It was the gift which suited her own active temperament and her own preferences. But now he has spoken. She has heard him say that maybe this is not the gift he really wants from her here and now. In her agitated state (the frustration must have been building up for some time before she finally confronted him directly about it), the mood in her kitchen must now be very dark indeed. Yet this apparently trivial incident is a real moment of grace in Martha's life: If she lives through it and is able to come to peace and get beneath the surface of her hurt feelings, she may become one of those rare souls who no longer merely work for God. She may begin instead to "do God's work."

Everything depends, though, on how Martha reacts. When prayer becomes dark, many good souls give up praying and lose themselves in work (which they find more congenial) for the Lord. When the work becomes frustrating, many good and zealous souls fail to see the Lord in the frustration. If they are very strong-willed, they merely charge ahead, taking all frustration as an obstacle to be overcome—an obstacle coming not from the Lord but from his "enemies." If they are more sensitive or more diffident, they give up the work, and perhaps spend their lives in hurt incomprehension, unable to understand why the Lord did not bless and look kindly on the gift they chose to give him. In neither case do they discover the real meaning of their frustration. They never realize that this dark hour is perhaps the most precious gift of their lives. It is an invitation to true poverty of spirit—to have no will of my own in all I do for love[9]—and as such it is the real beginning of eternal life.

The Martha of the gospels, it seems, was great-souled enough to learn the lesson and to remain with the Lord even as he journeyed to Calvary. But what a strange new world she must have entered that day in Bethany. Did she continue with the cooking? Or did she too drop everything and sit at the Lord's feet with Mary? Or are those really the wrong—the unimportant—questions to ask? Perhaps it is not so important *what* she did as *why* she did it.

[9] Cf. the Epilogue of *When the Well Runs Dry.*

Three

The Lord Likes "Blue Cheese"

*I*f Martha realized that the Lord's rebuke was really a great gift, a call to go deeper in her relationship with him, she still did not know precisely *how* she should change her ways of acting. When the difference between working for God and doing God's work began to dawn on her, she could see that the Lord was asking something radically new and different: Her accustomed ways of serving him were to be no longer sufficient or satisfactory and the frustration she encountered more and more frequently was to be taken as a clear sign of a call to grow.

Even this realization is itself a great gift. Normally it takes many frustrations and many dark days in the kitchen before we begin to suspect that the difficulties are the voice of God for us. At first we believe we must just push ahead, try harder, overcome the obstacles so as to get back to and get on with success in our apostolic work. We often tend to see these obstacles, as we said, as the work of the devil or of evil men impeding the work we are doing for God. And when the pattern of frustration becomes sufficiently marked—when prayerful people begin to realize that somehow the Lord is speaking in the difficulties—then we tend to feel that God is telling us that we have been deceiving ourselves, that all our efforts have been wasted all these years, that we have not really been loving and serving him as we thought. Our earlier sense of frustration gives way to a sense of failure; the frantic effort of Sisyphus to push the rock up the hill gives way to the feeling that the task is hopeless and we were misguided ever to attempt it.

As we saw in Chapter 2, this is a critical moment in the apostolic life. It corresponds to the interior crisis which we discussed in Chapter 4 of *When the Well Runs Dry,* the time when all our own activity in prayer seems (and certainly is) useless and inefficacious. Just as many pray-ers, according to St. John of the Cross, never get beyond that crisis point in prayer, so too, I suspect, many apostles[1] never discover the real depth of meaning behind the "darkness" which envelops their apostolic activity. This is why I suggested that it may not be so important *what* Martha did next after discouragement and frustration and hurt feelings darkened her kitchen. How she

---

[1] Recall that we use the word "apostle" here to mean all who are called to live an active response to their Christian faith "in the world." In this sense the married man or woman who experiences raising a family and working in a factory as his or her God-given vocation is as much an "apostle" as the religious teacher or the parish priest.

acted was not as significant as how she came to understand and accept the meaning, the message for her
which the darkness contained. What she really
needed most was *insight:* not a better way of acting
but a better way of seeing the meaning of the Lord's
rebuke. Action (and probably a new way of acting)
would follow upon her new way of seeing, of course.
But I believe that the new way of acting which was
called for would be evident enough once she understood the message of the Lord to her.

Let us suppose, then, that our Martha has survived
the stages of struggle and of discouragement and has
come to realize that there is a much deeper meaning
to the difficulties which block her efforts to work for
God. That is, she has begun to discover the difference
between working for God and doing God's work. She
has begun to suspect, however vaguely, that what
pleases him may not at all be what we think should
please him. And, while she finds it queer and somewhat repugnant that God should be a lover of blue
cheese, she is also becoming aware that her love for
him is stronger than her distaste for blue cheese.

Such an inversion of values, though, is probably far
in the future. Martha will probably find herself struggling to accept the cross, out of love, for a long, long
time before the day comes when she can embrace the
cross wholeheartedly. In fact, at this early stage of her
journey, talk of loving or embracing the cross would
likely strike her as repugnant and masochistic. This is
especially true today, when personal fulfillment and
self-affirmation are valued so highly. We want a
Christianity which is joyous, positive, Resurrection-
centered. We see as unhealthy any stress on penance

or suffering as ends in themselves. We are right in this, of course; as we saw in Chapter 5 of *Opening to God,* mortification, purification can never be more than means in a genuine following of Christ. God does not enjoy our misery. But what we may fail to realize today is that there is no other road to Easter Sunday except that which passes through Good Friday: Calvary is the only *means* to resurrection with Jesus Christ. He himself was very explicit about this: "If a man wishes to come after me, he must deny his very self, take up his cross, and begin to follow in my footsteps. Whoever would save his life will lose it, but whoever loses his life for my sake will find it" (Mt 16:24-25)—a proclamation which follows upon, and is provoked by, Peter's unwillingness to believe that Jesus could be serious in predicting his own crucifixion.

The crucial difference between Chapter 5 of *Opening to God* and our present discussion is this: There we were speaking about the *active* purification of the soul (what we do to dispose ourselves for God), whereas here we are speaking of what John of the Cross calls the *passive* purification, that is, what God does in us to transform us. We spoke of this passive purification in our *interior* lives in Chapters 4 and 5 of *When the Well Runs Dry.* There we saw that the darkness which assails and troubles the soul in prayer is really the blinding light of God penetrating into, and cauterizing, our sinful spirits. As St. John of the Cross often stresses, the very same light which, for the saints, is the direct vision of God, is a searing fire for souls still wounded by sin. The *active* purification of our souls—what *we* do to dispose ourselves to encounter God—corresponds to what we traditionally call asceticism. By contrast, the passive purification of contemplation is God's work in us: We are the patients of this Divine Surgeon, and the knife he wields is his own self-communication. Or, to return to our original metaphor, the intense light of his presence gradually but painfully drives out all the darkness of sin in us. In Chapters 4 and 5 of the *Well* we spoke of how this happens interiorly, in prayer; now we see that it takes place not only interiorly but in the external events and circumstances of our active lives as well. It was, indeed, this external passive purification in his own life to which Jesus was referring in the prediction of the passion just noted: "From then on Jesus (the Messiah) started to indicate to his disciples that he must go to Jerusalem and suffer greatly there at the hands of the leaders, the chief priests, and the scribes, and to be put to death, and raised up on the third day" (Mt 16:21). Perhaps Jesus did freely choose to "do penance," as for example when he fasted for 40 days at the beginning of his public life. Here, however, it is a question not of penance chosen but of "penance" imposed, at the hands of "the elders and chief priests and scribes," a passive purification which Jesus saw, and Peter failed to see, as being the will of God the Father for him.

We have spoken of this passive purification of our active, apostolic lives as "blue cheese" and as the cross, Calvary in our lives. The latter may seem too big, too dramatic for the ordinary lives of ordinary friends of God like ourselves. And "blue cheese" may seem too exotic an example to have much concrete application in most of our lives. So perhaps it would be good to spell out what we mean by giving some down-to-earth biblical examples.

One of the dominant themes of the whole Old Testament is the strangeness of the ways in which Yahweh chooses to accomplish his designs for Israel. More often than not these ways run counter to the efforts and the expectations even of his chosen instruments. Thus when Abram is given a new name, Abraham ("father of a multitide"), and is chosen to be the father of many nations, he and Sarah, his wife, are already very old and have long abandoned hope of ever having children. So far-fetched is the Lord's message that Abraham cannot take it seriously: "God further said to Abraham: 'As for your wife Sarai, do not call her Sarai; her name shall be Sarah. I will bless her, and I will give you a son by her. Him also will I bless; he shall give rise to nations, and rulers of peoples shall issue from him.' Abraham prostrated himself and laughed as he said to himself, 'Can a child be born to a man who is a hundred years old? Or can Sarah give birth at ninety?' " (Gn 17:15-17). Abraham even suggests to God that he fulfill his promises through Ishmael (his son by the Egyptian slave-girl Hagar) instead, since the promise of a son by Sarah seems impossible to fulfill. And when Sarah overhears the Lord's insistent promise of a son in their old age, she too can only laugh from behind the door of their tent (Gn 18:12). How could anyone seriously believe that God would work in this way?

The choice of David as King of Israel, while not quite so spectacular as the birth of Isaac, is equally contrary to the expectations of the chosen people, of his own family, and even of the prophet, Samuel, who was sent by Yahweh to anoint as king one of the sons of Jesse. Seven sons were presented to Samuel. "As they came, he looked at Eliab and thought, 'Surely the LORD'S anointed is here before him.' But the LORD said to Samuel: 'Do not judge from his appearance or from his lofty stature, because I have rejected him.' . . . Then Jesse called Abinadab and presented him before Samuel, who said, 'The LORD has not chosen him.'" (1 Sm 16:6-9). And so it went with all the rest of the seven. Jesse did not even think of presenting David, the youngest, since he was a mere boy, still tending his sheep. Yet it was David whom the Lord had chosen.

Not surprisingly, King Saul greatly resented David and the Lord's choice of him, since the anointing of David meant the end of his own family's claim to the throne. But even Eliab, David's own elder brother, could not accept the choice of this child as the anointed of Israel. Soon after the anointing, when Goliath and the Philistines were sowing terror in the hearts of all the Israelites, David came to the battlefield, sent by Jesse to see how his brothers and the Israelite army were faring in battle. He began to exhort the Israelites to fight bravely in the name of the Lord. And Eliab retorted: "Why did you come down? With whom have you left those sheep in the desert meanwhile? I know your arrogance and your evil intent. You came down to enjoy the battle!" (1 Sm 17:28). Yet, as we know so well, it was David, armed only with his slingshot and the power of God, who was to defeat the invincible giant, Goliath, and save Israel from mortal danger.

The whole history of David's reign—his protection from the jealousy of Saul; the terrible murder of Uriah because of David's lust for Bathsheba, Uriah's wife, who nonetheless became the mother of the great King Solomon; David's restoration to power after the attempted coup of his own son, Absalom— all of these events echo the strangeness of the designs and the works of Yahweh. When people attempt to frustrate the plans of God, their very evil acts often become the vehicle for the fulfillment of the divine plan. And when they attempt to promote the interests of Yahweh, their own well-intentioned efforts seem to come to nothing. Truly his ways are inscrutable, farther from the thoughts of men than are the heavens from the earth. He brings good out of the evil designs of men and women, and he often brings to naught their sincere efforts to do good according to their own lights. ·

If this were the whole point, however, of the story of Yahweh's dealings with Abraham and David, we would seem to be trapped in predestination or fatalism: a God who manipulates history to his own ends, irrespective of human intentions. And in the early biblical writings, indeed, such a deterministic picture of God does appear. But this is not the whole story; as Old Testament religion matures, it becomes clearer and clearer that God is not merely manipulating human beings like chess men on a board. He does not want to force his will on helpless creatures. Rather he seeks to win his people to free partnership in the work of redemption and sanctification. Abraham and Sarah laughed, but then they believed. And it was because of their *free* surrender to the paradoxical promises of God that Abraham became "the father of many nations." Paul says, paraphrasing Genesis 15:3, "Abraham believed God, and it was credited to him as justice" (Rom 4:3). Similarly, David allowed the Lord to work through his littleness and powerlessness. And even when he sinned with Bathsheba, he surrendered to the judgment of God pronounced through Nathan. When the child of their adultery died, David bowed to the Lord's just judgment, and only later was Solomon born as the promised heir to David's everlasting throne (2 Sm 12).

Examples could be multiplied indefinitely, but perhaps the point is clear. The author of the Epistle to the Hebrews summarizes it beautifully in a magnificent chapter on faith (chapter 11): "Faith," he says, "is confident assurance concerning what we hope for, and conviction about things we do not see. Because of faith the men of old were approved by God" (Heb 11:1-2). He then surveys the great Old Testament figures, from Abel to the prophets, in support of his contention that it was, in every instance, the faith of these chosen men and women which won their justification and secured the fulfillment of the divine promises for Israel. Yahweh led them where they could not reasonably expect, and often did not wish, to go. But it was their free "yes" to—their faith in—his mysterious will which made them a living part of the great flow of salvation history.[2]

I hope this brief reflection on the ways of the Lord in the lives of some of the great Old Testament

---

[2] As we shall see in Chapter 4, the same point is beautifully illustrated in the call of the great prophets. In every case (see especially Moses' objections in Exodus 3:11 and 4:1, 10 and 13, as well as Isaiah 6:1-8 and Jeremiah 1:4-10), the prophet is

figures makes clearer how the "blue cheese" of God plays a crucial role in the apostolic calling. As the author of Hebrews makes clear, too, their experience is very similar to our own. Their faith, in the face of the surprises and the darknesses of God, is precisely the faith which Martha needed in her kitchen. And which we too need if the Lord is to work in and through us today. What happened to Abraham must also happen to us, if we are to be fully the Lord's apostles and prophets—if it is to be his word, and not our own, which issues from our mouths.

How, concretely, does he accomplish this in us? As I reflected on this theme over the past year, it seemed to me that there are three main kinds of "darkness in the marketplace" in our active lives, each of which is intimately linked with the mystery of the dry well or dark night of our soul's journey to God. The first and most pleasant (once we accept it) we might call "having nothing to say or do." The second, much more painful, is the frustration and the rejection of our efforts, and even the questioning of our motives by good men and women despite our best efforts to serve. And the third, which I feel may be the deepest, is simply being overlooked and "accounted as nothing." Martha's experience when the

---

keenly aware of his own unworthiness and Yahweh makes clear that, if he accepts the call, the prophet will speak not by his own power but by the power of God at work in him:

Say not, "I am too young."
To whomever I send you, you shall go;
whatever I command you, you shall speak.
Have no fear before them,
because I am with you to deliver you, says the LORD
(Jer 1:7-8).

Lord rebuked her appears to be an example of the second kind of darkness; and Calvary itself would seem to be of this kind too. It is the most dramatic of the three, and is probably what most of us would think of when we reflect on the darkness in our own lives. But each of the three is important and each deepens and transforms us in a different way. So, in the chapters that follow, let us take each in turn and see what we can discover of the Lord's mysterious ways.

Part Two

Four

The Readiness of the Unready

As I mentioned earlier, for some years I have been teaching a course on discernment of spirits. The name is probably somewhat mysterious and obscure to the average pray-er, although in recent years discernment has enjoyed a renaissance among theologians and spiritual writers. Basically, as I see it, "discernment" may be defined as the meeting point of prayer and action. That is, discernment is the art of recognizing what God is asking of us—what he would like us to do with our lives, how he wishes us to respond to the concrete life-situations which we encounter in following our vocation. It is thus a more technical term for what all committed pray-ers are seeking when they "pray for guidance." It is called discernment *of spirits* because, as we noted in Chapter 2, our war is not merely against flesh and blood, but against "principalities and powers" (Eph 6:12). Thus there are opposing "spirits," God and the devil, seeking to speak to our hearts and to guide our lives. And since the devil is a fraud who speaks as "an angel of light" (2 Cor 11:14), it takes considerable experience to judge correctly *who* is speaking to our inner selves and what we are being led to do. It is this judgment, rooted in experience, which we call discernment.

We mentioned before that discernment is very concrete: It is not a question of discovering what is right or wrong in general or in the abstract, but of discovering what God is asking of me in this very specific and concrete situation in which I find myself now. It is not a question, for example, whether social justice is an essential part of any Christian vocation; nor even, to take a further specification of the general obligation to practice social justice, whether priests and religious should involve themselves in politics as a way to promote social justice today. These questions are of utmost importance in the Christian life; the recent popes have all spoken to them and have attempted to formulate the authentic application of Jesus' gospel teaching to these crucial questions. Discernment enters in not at the level of principle but at the consequent level of concrete action—of specific decisions by souls committed to live by the principles given by the Lord to guide the Christian life. As we noted in *Opening to God*,[1] the guidance of legitimate authority can never free the mature Christian from

---

[1] Chapter 3: "The Relevance of Prayer: Discernment." I pointed out there (p. 46) that St. Thomas Aquinas is one great authority for the distinction between authoritative teaching on the general principles of a moral life and the discerning process whereby these principles are applied to specific concrete decisions.

the need and the responsibility to make discerning choices in his or her own life. For example, a priest or religious guided by the social-involvement principles indicated in the preceding paragraph, would still have to ask: "What then should *I* be doing in *this* parish (or this school), with *these* people and *these* very real situations of social injustice?" While the papal and conciliar teachings on the question are much more detailed than I have indicated, our committed apostle would normally not find a complete, detailed answer to this specific question, even if he or she became fully conversant with all the church documents. The best proof of this, I suppose, is that truly committed and knowledgeable churchmen and churchwomen still disagree about the proper way for them to handle the crucial social questions of our day.

Thus, to summarize our discussion so far, discernment enters into our life as the immediate guide to concrete action. It seeks to answer the question: Granted all the principles which the gospel and the church give me as guides, how does the Lord wish me to apply them to act concretely, here and now? Sometimes the answer may be clear; for example, when a religious is given a specific and legitimate task or mission by one whom she has vowed to obey; or when a mother of a family is called in the night to care for her sick husband or sick child. In such situations, they would scarcely need to "discern" what God wishes of them here and now, anymore than I would normally need to discern whether to celebrate Mass for my congregation at the assigned time.

But there are many instances in our lives where God's will is not so clear, even granted a clear grasp of, and firm commitment to, the demands of our vocation. And, to return now to the "darkness in the marketplace" situation which is the theme of this book, I believe these obsure situations will become more, and not less, common the more we grow in union with God. I believe, that is, that the darkness and dryness of our prayer will find an echo in the obscurity of our perception of the Lord's apostolic will for us. At first this might be surprising; people would normally assume, I suppose, that the closer we are to God the more clearly we sense his desires and think his thoughts—just as they would normally assume that "deep" pray-ers lead untroubled inner lives of ecstasies and consolations. We have already noted, however, in Part 2 of *When the Well Runs Dry,* that the latter assumption is quite mistaken.[2] I am afraid the former is equally erroneous.

When I was teaching my course on discernment last year, one of my students asked a question which has caused me to reflect much on this topic. She is a member of the Society of Our Lady of the Way, one of the new secular institutes with which the church has been blessed only in the past 40 years. The members of the secular institutes form a bridge between the traditional religious life and the lay life. They have vows and are committed to a celibate life, and yet generally they live at home and work in ordinary jobs. Their apostolate is an anonymous one (they have no distinctive dress), an insertion into the ordi-

[2] See Chapter 3, above (pp. 55-56), for a summary description of the troubles of those who begin to draw near to the Light of God.

nary life and work situations which priests and religious would rarely encounter. Since their workmates do not usually know of their vowed status, they see people "with their hair down," whereas we priests normally see them on their good behavior. Thus the members of these new secular institutes are "in the marketplace" in a very thoroughgoing way. There are many such institutes in the church today. The Society of Our Lady of the Way, however, was founded by a Jesuit in Vienna, and its spirituality is very close to that of the Society of Jesus to which I belong. This means that the members are called, as are we Jesuits, to be "contemplatives in action," to live a life in which all, apostolic involvement as well as formal prayer, is contemplation. To use a pregnant phrase of St. Ignatius Loyola, they are called to "seek God in all things." There is a breaking down of the traditional monastic wall separating the prie-dieu from the marketplace.

Such a life is beautiful in theory but difficult in practice. When we come to speak of the prayer experience of the dry well or the dark night it becomes even more problematic. It was precisely this difficulty which gave rise to my friend's question. She said something like this: "If we are called to be 'contemplatives in action'—to seek and find God not only in formal prayer but in all our apostolic works—what happens when we are in the dark night of formal prayer? When God seems far away and we seem to know nothing of him or his ways? What then do we have to 'give' to others, or to 'respond to' in our ministry? How can we find him in all things when we seem to have lost him in prayer? It seems our ministry will also be—or appear to be—useless and empty."

I don't know how much my reply to her question (which was written at the end of one of her assignment papers) helped her then. But the question itself has been one of the main signposts by which the Lord pointed me to the writing of this book. It led me to a much more thoroughgoing exploration of the link, if any, between the dry well of our prayer and the dark marketplace of our work for the Lord. And it pointed up a difficulty in integrating prayer and action which has been experienced by apostles in every age, and which is barely hinted at in the beautiful but obscure phrase, "contemplative in action." Let us try to describe how this difficulty emerges in the lives of maturing pray-ers.

When we first begin to experience the dry well in our prayer, it will often happen that our work will be quite fruitful and fulfilling. When people come to me for direction in the early stages of the dry well or the dark night, they usually say that they are happy in their vocation, fulfilled in their work and blessed with good and supportive friends. In fact, this basic sense of well-being in their outer world is what makes the inner darkness and dryness all the more puzzling to them. God's apparent silence or absence is difficult to reconcile with the apostolic fulfillment they find. I have learned that this apparent contradiction between their inner and outer lives is one of the surest signs that their experience of dryness is really a healthy sign of growth. If there is much external disturbance and unhappiness, I would first assume that this was somehow the cause of their interior difficulties and would expect that remedying the marketplace situation would probably bring back the prie-dieu experience of the Lord. As St. Thomas taught us long ago, we don't look for supernatural explanations when there are natural causes at hand to explain our experience.

It makes sense, too, that the Lord would work this way in the beginning. If there were darkness at every level of our lives at the same time, most beginners would be overwhelmed by discouragement and give up. As we grow stronger, though, and more at home with the inner darkness, it is equally sensible that what is happening within us would tend to "overflow" into our apostolic lives. Even then, the darkness within and the darkness without will often not be simultaneous, but alternating. That is, for many years we will probably find that the times of apostolic success and consolation are times of inner dryness and, conversely, when things are difficult externally we will be sustained and supported by a strong inner sense of God's love and presence. This alternation corresponds to the alternating periods of inner light and darkness which we described in Chapter 3 of *When the Well Runs Dry.* We said there that it is by means of this alternation that the Lord leads us into the passive prayer of contemplation. He gently teaches us, by means of the unpredictable rhythm of his presence and absence, to let him be the boss in our prayer. Similarly here, the rhythmic alternation of apostolic and contemplative fruitfulness and apparent fruitlessness teaches us—called to be contemplatives in action—to let him be the boss of our whole life. If one is to become a true contemplative in action, then the Lord must take over all of his or her life and experience: the inner and the outer (prie-dieu and marketplace). Eventually this may mean that both will be dark by our standards of light and darkness; but the Lord is gentle enough, and concerned enough for our growth, not to bring about this "total eclipse" unless and until we are ready for it.

Now my friend's question may make more sense to us. When the prayer is dark, what happens in the apostolate? Various things may happen. Sometimes—often in the early days—the apostolate, our active lives, will be quite fruitful *and* joyous. We will find it strange, because the inner darkness means that we have come to depend on the Lord as the source and cause of our success, and it seems odd that apostolic success comes even though he is apparently absent within. Since we have come to depend on prayer to sustain and enlighten us (this is the fruit of the long early years of learning to pray by drawing water from the well of meditation and imaginative contemplation[3]), we naturally expect that we will have nothing to give once the well of prayer has dried up. But we find this is not the case. Despite our painful sense of having nothing to give, others seem to be helped by what we do and touched by what we say.

This "readiness of the unready" to benefit others is profoundly mysterious. I know it has often sur-

---

[3] See Chapter 6 of *Opening to God* and Chapters 1 and 2 of *When the Well Runs Dry*. In the last-named chapter we stressed that the water (consolation) of prayer is precisely for the flowers of the virtues in our lives.

prised me in my own life, and I have found my own experience repeated often in the lives of my directees. Even in the early days I can now see, with hindsight, some hint of what was to come. How often I labored over a sermon, and delivered it with great care and feeling, only to have someone tell me later how much they had been helped by something I had not even planned to say, or perhaps was not even aware I had said. This disturbed me at first: I wanted to say, "But what about all the beautiful insights I labored to present? Didn't you notice them?" Gradually, however, I began to catch on to the joke the Lord was playing on me. And I was able to laugh at myself for thinking my own efforts and eloquence were so important to the work of grace. When many of the seminarians, as they matured in prayer, shared their own identical experience with me, the point became clearer.

At the same time, the darkness-with-fruitfulness became more marked in my own life. As the son of a man who wore both a belt and suspenders at the same time, I have always tended to be thoroughly prepared for everything. Yet more and more often I found myself paralyzed interiorly when I tried to prepare to preach a sermon or give a talk on prayer. In the seminary, we rise early and have our "meditation" and Mass before breakfast. The various faculty members take turns as the principal celebrant and homilist at the liturgy. And so, when it was my turn, I would reflect on the day's readings during the community's meditation time in order to discover what the Lord wanted me to share with the seminarians. Gradually, however, it became impossible to "think" during that prayer time. I found it a very frustrating experience, given my organized nature, and struggled to collect my thoughts. The dryness and darkness had become acceptable to me in my personal, private prayer. And I had even learned to accept the fact that what helped others might not be what I had so carefully prepared. But still it went against the grain to be actually "unprepared" when I was to preach to others. Yet now the struggle seemed fruitless. I just could not think a coherent thought.

What finally made me realize, after much complaining to the Lord, that this was really his will and his way was that the sermons I gave in this state were the ones that really hit home for the seminarians. I could not say that I enjoyed this deeper "readiness of the unready"—not for a long time anyway—but I did begin to feel sure it was really what the Lord wanted. And I could appreciate the humbling value of it. In fact, I believe it was at this time that the Old Testament passages which describe the calls of the prophets became very precious to me. The best-known are perhaps Exodus 3 and 4 (the call of Moses), Isaiah 6:1-8 and Jeremiah 1:4-10. In each case the prophet protests his own unworthiness to be Yahweh's messenger: Moses stammers, Isaiah is a man of unclean lips, Jeremiah is "just a youth." But their very human inadequacy seems to be what draws Yahweh to choose them. He told Jeremiah, in response to his protests, "See, I place my words in your mouth!" It seemed to be an equally true description of what he wanted to do in me, if only I could let my mind and my mouth be empty of my own well-meaning but conflicting words.

As I began to realize this and to try to cooperate with what the Lord was doing (although even now there are times when I am tempted to think I am just being lazy), the results more than confirmed the correctness of my discernment. In addition, I have since seen the same phenomenon in the experience of many of my directees. It seems to be a clear illustration, at the apostolic level, of that superiority of floating over swimming which we discussed in Chapter 6 of *When the Well Runs Dry,* and to which we will return in Chapter 5 (pp. 94, 100-101) and in the Epilogue (pp. 123-124, 126-128) of the present book. Since we humans are very manipulative, it never becomes really easy to do; but the results make clear that it is the best way if only we can muster the faith to let the Lord take over.

It is perhaps good to stress that I am not urging a policy of deliberate unpreparedness. All of the great Christian masters of prayer insist, when speaking of "passive" or infused prayer, that we should continue to be meditators—to actively seek the Lord by our own reflection, acts of the will, vocal prayer—as long as we are able to do so. To seek to force passivity and self-emptying would be to anticipate grace. The dry well or dark night in prayer is God's free gift, totally beyond our human achieving or meriting, and we should wait humbly on the Lord and be happy to trod the natural paths as long as he wishes us to do so.[4]

---

[4] St. Teresa of Avila is a very good guide here. See especially Chapter 3 of the Fifth Mansion of *The Interior Castle,* where she says that the only union essential to holiness is the union of my will with God's, and this union is possible (at least in theory) even if the soul *never* in this life experiences the infused contemplation of the dry well. Similarly, the author of *The Cloud of*

Similarly, it would be presumptuous and offensive to the Lord were we to fail to prepare to proclaim his word, or do his work, while it is still possible for us to do our part. But, as in prayer so too in ministry, the time may well come when we cannot do anything and yet, in ways we don't understand, something is done in us and through us. It is this fruitful apostolic paralysis which I have called "the readiness of the unready." It is, I think, the first of the three kinds of darkness in the marketplace.

The experience I have described is my own (and that of many others) as a pray-er. For example, at times I am going to preach or teach—to proclaim the Lord's word to his people—and yet all is blank when I seek to discern, in prayer, what he wishes me to say or to do. It is as if he were saying: "You just be still and empty and loving. Let me worry about what I will say or do through you." And despite my reluctant unreadiness, I find myself ready when the right moment comes. Two other experiences also strike me as being of this type; both are my own, but they have been abundantly confirmed by the experiences of others whom I have directed.

One experience pertains to my work precisely as a spiritual director. As I think I have indicated, the heart of spiritual direction is discernment. The directee comes to the director to hear God speak to him or her: It is a sacramental situation. Yet, it is not a mechanical pronouncement of divine decrees from

---

Unknowing warns the disciple for whom he writes not to give the book to anyone unless it is clear the Lord himself has begun to lead the person along the way of "unknowing" or infused contemplation.

on high. The primary discerner of God's word is the directee himself or herself. The director is, as I see it, an interpreter, a co-discerner. Together they seek to hear and understand the Lord's loving word. In this context, it is usually helpful to explain to the directee why I discerned his or her situation as I did; that is, to give the reasons which lead me to conclude that the experience is (or is not) from the "good spirit." In this way, directees are able to understand better what is happening in their lives, and they will be able to discern more confidently and more accurately for themselves in the future. Yet, I have often found myself feeling or sensing that their experiences were (or were not) genuinely from God, without being able to say precisely why. That is, without having any reason for so judging, I feel I "just know" which spirit is at work in the directee's life, in what is being shared with me. Often this happens in a situation of friendship and implicit trust, and there is no problem for the directee in accepting my instinctive judgment. But if he or she finds it difficult to accept, I in turn find myself at a loss to explain further.

This type of "readiness of the unready" has been a very beautiful part of my experience as a director. It always reminds me of an incident early in my priestly life, when I was a graduate student at the University of Notre Dame in Indiana. At that time, several of the graduate student sisters on campus used to come to me for direction. It was the period, in the late 1960s, when religious life changed drastically—from the monastery to the marketplace almost overnight, one might say. Even sisters from still "conservative" communities found themselves much more on their own, much more free at Notre Dame. And the sister of whom I am speaking was from a very traditional background. Yet, as we shared, it became clearer that the real problem was not religious structures but faith itself.[5] The uncertainties of the time forced her to confront the abyss of faith. She was a beautifully honest person, very direct and sincere. Thus I was nonplussed when she said to me one day: "Let me ask you just one question: Is God really real for you?" After hesitating a long moment, I said, "Yes. I'm sure he is. But I don't know how I can prove it to you." Her answer surprised and humbled me. "No, that's not necessary," she said. "As long as I know that he is real to you, that is reason enough for me to continue searching."

The readiness of the unready! I learned a lesson that day about how the Lord might choose to work through me, a lesson I have never forgotten. I don't

[5] As I look back, I think the real crisis of this momentous age was, and is, a crisis of faith. In the past the raw risk and Kierkegaardian "uncertainty" of faith was masked, and even evaded, by the elaborate religious structures within which we lived and moved. When these structures were questioned, and often removed, all of us were confronted with the frightening realization that our faith may have been in the structures (comfortable and certain and familiar) and not in the all-holy and mysterious God "behind" the structures. If St. John of the Cross is correct (see *The Ascent of Mount Carmel,* Book III, especially Chapters 33-45), this frightening realization may be the greatest grace of our age: It would be the beginning of a "dark night" for the church, by which we would be drawn to encounter God himself and not just our images of God. Of course, the ultimate outcome depends on our willingness to risk the dark; we can, if we wish, cling to our comfortable images and structures, or merely replace those that are lost with new images and structures. The new may be better than the old; but they are still just images, and not the living God!

know whether my sister-friend ever found what she was searching for, and we have not been in touch for many years. But I thank her for the lesson I learned that day. I pray for her now, as I have often done, that her honesty be abundantly rewarded by the Lord she sought.

The final type of experience that seems to me to embody this readiness of the unready of which we speak is what I have called "the accidents of God." As I look back on my own life, it seems that the most important turning points were not only unplanned by me but were actually contrary to what I intended and expected. At the time, it seemed that events were frustrating the plans I had (and presumed the Lord had) for my serving him and doing his will. Only by hindsight can I see the providence at work in these apparently frustrating "accidents." But now they seem to form the real unifying thread of my life, a thread which runs from my sudden and unexpected entry into the Jesuits only five or six weeks after my first serious contact with them, right down to the present day. One or two examples, which are particularly striking for me, might help to make the point clearer. The idea, of course, is not to burden you, the reader, with my own life story, but to help you to reflect on the same pattern in your own life. For I truly believe that it is precisely these "accidents of God" which turn swimmers into floaters and workers for God into those who do God's work. He teaches us to let go even though we cling blindly to our own plans and ideas.

During our novitiate days, our master of novices was a man with a truly missionary heart. When I became a Jesuit I had, as far as I can recall, no idea of becoming a missionary. But this man, who never went to the missions himself, filled us with a sense of the missionary life as the fulfillment of the Jesuit ideal of service to the church. St. Francis Xavier was a heroic figure for him, and the enthusiasm was contagious. Thus it was not surprising that I found myself volunteering for the missions. When the superior general of the Jesuits requested volunteers for the Japanese mission (just beginning to recover from the ravages of war), it seemed natural that I should offer myself. The Philippines was the mission assigned to the New York Province, while Japan was an international mission. But since the superior general said the need was greatest in Japan, I volunteered to go there. Soon I learned I was accepted for Japan. This meant I could not leave for the missions as soon as my classmates assigned to the Philippines (where English was the lingua franca). Since I would need two years to learn Japanese, I was told I would have to stay behind and finish college and my M.A. in the United States before going to language school in Japan. So I stayed behind. I read all I could find on Japan, and even learned a few words of Japanese (and also encountered a great spiritual director). And then, as my studies were nearing an end, my superior called me to tell me I was going to the Philippines! No reasons were given; only years later did I learn the reason for the change, and it merely deepened my wonder at how God writes straight with crooked lines. I certainly had no objections to going to the Philippines. Indeed, the 24 years that have passed since that day have made me count my assignment to that lovely land one of the great blessings of my life. But at the time it certainly seemed like a very peculiar way to run a horse race!

Little did I realize that the pattern set then was to be repeated over and over again: my assignment to graduate studies in the philosophy of science; the later assignment to San Jose Seminary; and finally, my assignment to teach courses in spirituality and discernment (very far, it would seem, from the philosophy of science), an assignment which eventually led to the writing of three books. These "accidents of God" became, as I have said, the crucial turning points in my life up to now. Indeed, as I wonder what tomorrow may bring, I find now I almost expect the unexpected. And when students have asked me lately what would be the best preparation for a ministry of spiritual direction, I have said, only half-jokingly, "a degree in the philosophy of science"![6]

As I look back over these pages, I feel somewhat uncomfortable to find so much of "I" and "me" there. True confessions have never been to my taste. But maybe that is the only way to put flesh and blood on the bones of our ideas. I would hope that my sharing

[6] Strange as the yoking of philosophy of science and spirituality may seem, I really believe the former has helped me immensely with the latter. The empirical, experiential, hypothetical training I received has profoundly affected my whole approach to the interior life. I find myself very wary of grand conceptual schemes, of fitting people into mental boxes. Theories are fine, in spirituality as in service, but only if they begin from experience and return to experience for their ultimate verification. The fact that my doctoral mentor, Father Ernan McMullin, is not only a renowned philosopher of science but also a real man of God has doubtless had much to do with the "marriage" of the two areas in my own life and thinking.

might move each reader to look into his or her life to discover there the patterns of God's working in this first kind of darkness in the marketplace. What I have tried to share is the three kinds of "readiness of the unready" which I have discovered in my own life: as a pray-er, when I am going to preach or teach, and I go to prayer for guidance only to find everything "blank" and the Lord seemingly asking that he just be free to say whatever he wishes through me; as a director, when I feel or sense what is right for the directee, and yet cannot say why it is right or give reasons for my judgment; and as an apostle, in the turning points of my life, when it seems to be the "accidents of God" which lead in the right, though unexpected and often unwanted, direction.

These may not be the only instances of the readiness of the Lord's unready. But they do make clear the pattern of that first kind of darkness in the marketplace. In recent years I have sometimes thought of my life as a large room or corridor, with many closed doors leading off the corridor. As I try the doors, some are locked; but others, often less promising looking, open easily. The locked doors are not to be opened, at least by me. But the ones that do open lead to new doors—and new surprises. If I persist in struggling with the locked doors, the whole experience can be very frustrating. But if I try the doors with an open, receptive spirit, not forcing the locks but exploring fully what lies beyond the un-locked ones—if I am happy with the fact that it is the Lord who holds the keys—then my whole life can become an exciting and wonderful journey through the rooms he has chosen for me.

Five

For Better or Worse

*A*t the end of Chapter 3, I noted that I had discovered three kinds of darkness in the marketplace of our active lives, once we begin to live interiorly the dry well or dark night. The first of these, which we have discussed in Chapter 4, is what I have called "the readiness of the unready." The darkness there is not a sense of apostolic frustration or failure, but rather an experience of apostolic effectiveness without our understanding why or how it happens. It is a darkness of obscurity—not of pain and failure and frustration. That is why I mentioned in Chapter 3 that it is perhaps the most "pleasant" of the three kinds of apostolic darkness.

There is, of course, an initial anxiety even here. To preach without knowing what one is going to say is certainly unnerving for anyone who takes his or her vocation seriously. Or to direct souls without being able to explain the basis for one's "intuitive" judgment as to the spirits at work. Or to find one's best efforts to plan and prepare repeatedly upended by the "accidents of God." These situations are unnerving, and many good souls probably never do discover and accept the real meaning of them for their ministry. But if we do understand what is happening, and are able to respond by hanging loose, letting go, floating free, then we learn to live in a marketplace darkness which is not disturbing but joyous. After all, the sermons do help others; the intuitive judgments of direction do prove correct in the subsequent experience of the directee; and the accidents of God do prove to be far more fruitful than all our plans and hopes. Losing control is initially difficult to accept, but the results more than justify the risk.

We said in Chapter 3, though, that this is only the first kind of darkness in the apostolic marketplace of our active life. The second kind is much more painful. I described it there as "the frustration and rejection of our efforts, and even the questioning of our motives by good men and women, despite our best efforts to serve" the Lord and his people. This kind of darkness means not only obscurity but apparent failure. It is far more painful than the readiness of the unready, and far more sanctifying in the end. It is, indeed, the passion in our lives: "In my own flesh I fill up what is lacking in the sufferings of Christ" (see Col 1:24). But even those words do not capture the pain of the experience. Paul wrote them toward the end of his life, and he says in the verse cited, "I find my joy in the suffering I endure for you." He had not, however, always been so joyous about his suffering, or so clear about its deeper meaning. Some years earlier, when he wrote Second Corinthians, he was far more anguished in his description of the suffering he experienced, a suffering not only *for* the Corinthians but *caused by* their own attitude toward him.[1] Here Paul reflects much more the anguish of Gethsemane than the triumphant joy in the suffering of Calvary and in his own letter to the Colossians. Suffering in itself is not devastating. But when God seems absent, and we are not sure that we are on his side, then the pain can be beyond description—the greater the more his love has become the only light of our lives. I suspect that the link between the inner and the outer, between the prie-dieu and the marketplace, becomes much stronger at this point. That is, I believe the *pain* of the darkness of mature prayer is much more likely to come principally from outside ourselves, from the world in which we are called to live our purification, rather than from the purely interior trials of the soul. Since I have come to this belief only gradually and confusedly, let me try to explain further why I feel the marketplace is normally the source of this suffering and pain.

I mentioned in the *Well* that we can, and should, gradually learn to be at home in the inner darkness of prayer. Once we do learn to float gracefully, the darkness is no longer a desolating experience; the anxiety and turmoil of the soul in the dark night come

---

[1] See especially chapters 7 to 13, where Paul is wrestling with many conflicting emotions: justifying his apostolic mission; assuring the Corinthians of his fidelity and love; rebuking them for their fickleness; even defending himself against criticism about his personal appearance and unimpressive preaching style. He seems, in a moment of desolation, to have been seeking to reassure himself as much as to convince them!

not from the darkness itself but from our failure to understand and accept the darkness as the normal way of purification and transformation. We fear that we have lost God just when his love has become all-important to us. How many times directees have said to me, "I wouldn't mind the dryness and the inability to 'pray,' if I were sure it is God's will for me. What really distresses me is the fear that it may be my own fault, that I may be displeasing him and causing his absence by my own sinfulness." It takes months to convince such souls that they are really on the right track. But once they do believe that it is truly God working this purifying dryness and darkness in them, and once they understand something of the reasons for the experience as we described them in Chapters 4 and 5 of the *Well,* they find themselves at peace, at home in the dark. Then the experience of darkness is no longer an experience of desolation. It is, in fact, a form of consolation, since there is peace and a deeper joy in the midst of the darkness. It is that "loving attentiveness" of which St. John of the Cross speaks in describing the proper attitude of the soul once the dark night sets in.[2]

[2] *The Ascent of Mount Carmel,* Book II, Chapter 12, #8 and Chapter 14, #6; also, and especially, *The Dark Night of the Soul,* Book I, Chapter 10, #4. In the *Ascent,* this "loving attentiveness" is simply contrasted with "meditation" and could be taken to mean just letting go of our own efforts to reflect, and being content to be before the Lord in wordless love. But in *The Dark Night,* where John is talking about the painful awareness of God's absence which marks the night of sense, he says to "pay no attention to discursive meditation, since this is not the time for it. They should allow the soul to remain in rest and quietude, even though it may seem very obvious to them that they are doing nothing and wasting time, and even though they

Once this dark loving attentiveness becomes possible and real to us, there is inner tranquillity even in the dark night. What happens then? There will still be moments when doubt and anxiety beset us, and when we feel we are again drowning in the sea of God's absence. But they are usually as brief as they are intense—sudden reminders that our peace is sheer gift and that nothing in us can possibly merit God's love for us. Then the dark peace returns. I am not completely sure why the Lord works this way. John says that the weakness of our human nature requires that these "edge of the abyss" experiences be brief, and that the Lord never tests us beyond our strength. I suspect, also, that they become briefer and less frequent because the very experience of darkness is gradually detaching us from all the sense stimuli which disturb our peace. As our attachments are cut one by one (although it takes a lifetime of love to complete the process) there is less and less which can disturb our souls. Somehow we become ever more

---

think this disinclination to think about anything is due to their laxity . . . . All that is required of them here is freedom of soul . . . . They must be content simply with a loving and peaceful attentiveness to God, and live without the concern, without the effort, and without the desire to taste and feel him. All these desires disquiet and distract it. . . ." (Book I, Chapter 10, #4, p. 317 in Kavanaugh and Rodriquez's translation). Here, in contrast to the reference in the *Ascent*, there is anxiety and disturbance (i.e., desolation) and the "loving attentiveness" of which John speaks is much harder to achieve; the soul feels that God is far away and John's advice to be lovingly attentive seems at first impossible to follow! (See also *The Living Flame of Love*, stanza III, paragraphs 33 and 65, where John discusses the later, more mature experience of the soul when even this loving attentiveness must be abandoned.)

certain that the Lord loves us just as we are, and that he has taken full responsibility for healing in us whatever blocks love. The inner serenity which this certainty brings is one of the greatest gifts of the dry well: If he accepts me totally as I am, what then can I possibly fear or be disturbed about? "If God is for us, who can be against us?" (Rom 8:31). Gradually this triumphant affirmation of Paul becomes our own response to all the doubts that seek to assail us in the darkness of the soul's night.

As I mentioned, though, this peace and confidence even in the midst of darkness is a fragile thing, in the sense that it can be destroyed in an instant if the Lord withdraws his peace-giving hand. It is a mysterious peace even at its best, since it resides in the very center of the soul and not on the "surface." This surface is our sense life, and the senses never fully enjoy perfect peace in this life. As the dry well or dark night becomes our usual experience in prayer, the senses play less of a role, and eventually virtually no role at all, in our prayer. Thus in prayer itself, except for the occasional "edge of the abyss" experiences which I mentioned above, there is not much room for the senses to seek to disturb the deeper peace of our souls. That is why I said, a few pages back, that I believe that the pain and desolation of our lives will rarely come in prayer proper as we grow. We accept the darkness; we are at peace with the purifying absence of God, and with our own sinfulness which we now realize only he can heal. What then can trouble us in prayer itself?

Yet we are not free of all trouble and disturbance. And I think this is where the "marketplace" (whether it be the community life of a cloistered contemplative or the family life of a harried parent) begins to play a more prominent role in the purifying passion of our lives. I said that I believe that the pain of the darkness of mature prayer is now more likely to come from the world in which we live, rather than from the interior trials of the soul. Perhaps the foregoing paragraphs will make it easier to understand why this is so. Normally real desolation involves our senses, and the faculties—understanding, imagination, memory—which are closely linked to our sense life. In the dark night of prayer these faculties and senses gradually fade out of the picture. They play virtually no part in the prayer of "loving attentiveness" which involves simply being the (often dumb and unfeeling) clay in the Potter's hands. Thus there is little room for desolation to enter in at the prie-dieu.[3]

But, by contrast, we reach the marketplace of our lives only through our senses. We can preach, teach, share, encourage, learn and love humanly only by means of our eyes and tongues and ears. Where the senses enter in, so too can the devil; and where he can come, so too can pain and desolation. The marketplace can be troubled even when the chapel is at peace.

---

[3] St. John of the Cross explains that the devil (who is *always* the cause of desolation according to St. Ignatius) can only touch our senses and those faculties which are linked to sense; he has no idea what is happening deeper in the soul, nor can he intervene there. This is why I have told many souls they should be happy if they cannot grasp what is happening within them. If they cannot grasp it, neither can the devil, and they are perfectly safe!

Concretely this means that we will still encounter frustration and failure in our work even when we have come to be at home in the darkness of prayer. We will, in the first place, find it difficult to establish a common ground with people who view life purely naturalistically. Once the Lord has become very real and important to us, it will be difficult, if not impossible, to communicate with people to whom he means little or nothing. This is painful, since these people may be humanly close to us—family or long-time friends. But this is not really the principal pain of which I speak in this chapter. Those who float in the sea of God will indeed find it difficult to share with those on the shore for whom the sea is unreal. But the deeper pain will arise when the swimmers and the floaters (both of whom have discovered the sea) find communication and mutual understanding difficult. Both those who "work for God" (the swimmers) and those who "do God's work" (the floaters) are involved with God and have somehow centered their lives on him. This makes it much harder to accept, or even to understand, whatever miscommunication and misunderstanding may arise. Why should our values and lifestyles conflict when we are both committed to the same Lord?

If I can trust my own experience and that of those I have directed, this alienation from those we serve, and even from our fellow workers in the Lord, is the greatest part of that marketplace darkness which I have called the passion in our lives. I do not make light of physical suffering, or of the frustrations which can, and always do, arise from the material circumstances of our lives: the worry about paying the bills in lean times; the job which makes us feel we are watering a dry stick and cannot escape the futility; the nagging illness which drains our energy and frustrates our plans. All of these are indeed a part of the purifying darkness. But for one who has said "yes" to God even to accepting the dry well of prayer, I doubt that any of these disturbances "cut very deep." They may obsess and distress us on our low days, but when we regain our balance they seem a small enough return of love for what the Lord endured for us in his own human life. As someone has said, "We can bear any 'how,' if only we have a 'why' for bearing it." Perhaps the point was made most graphically in an old and classic poster for Boys' Town: A young boy is seen carrying his even younger brother who has been crippled by polio, and the caption says: "He ain't heavy. He's my brother!"

But what if the brother we are carrying is not at all appreciative of our efforts to help him? What if he does not want to be helped, does not admit that he is crippled? A kicking, cursing cripple may well be very heavy indeed, even if he is my brother! And if I too am a cripple, he can easily say, "Who are you to carry me? What makes you think you are any better than I?" Of course he is right: In the realm of the spirit we are all cripples.

We mentioned in the *Well* that one of the surest signs of growth in the interior life is a growing awareness of our own sinfulness. This is especially true once our prayer becomes "contemplative," that is, receptively passive. When this dark night sets in, the soul is ever more conscious of the immense contrast between the holy light of God and its own sinful darkness. If this sin-consciousness is from God it is always, as we said, marked by a mysterious but deep peace. But it is a fragile peace which the devil is ever ready to disturb. We see our sinfulness and God's holiness, and we see no reason for him to love us. In fact, the more we grow, the less reasonable, humanly speaking, does it seem that he should or could love us. We are like a slum girl courted by a prince. When he is present and manifesting his love, the contrast between their backgrounds and cultures is very real but it seems to be swept away, rendered unimportant, by the force of his love. But when she is alone, and especially when she is in her own environment and among her own people, it is very easy to doubt even the possibility of the prince's loving her. Isn't such a marriage doomed from the start? There will be many friends to tell her it is. After all, you can take the girl out of the slum, but you can never, they will say, take the slum out of the girl. Even when the prince returns to listen to her doubts and reassure her of his love, she will wonder if his love can really last once he discovers what it means to live a whole lifetime with someone like her.

If the prince also tells her that he not only loves her, but that he wants her to be the channel of his love for her fellow slum dwellers—if he wants her to remain in the slum and not to escape to the palace where she could erase her past and give all her energies to learning to be a worthy consort of the prince—then the tension between her two worlds will become greater and greater for her. Even if she herself learns to live gracefully between two worlds, she remains a threat to those who only know the slum and don't wish to know anything else. And even those who dream of escaping the slum will very likely resent taking help from one of their own kind.

Jesus himself seems to have encountered this very problem in his life. All three of the synoptics record what must have been one of the saddest days of his public life: "He departed from there and returned to his own part of the country followed by his disciples. When the sabbath came he began to teach in the synagogue in a way that kept his large audience amazed. They said: 'Where did he get all this? What kind of wisdom is he endowed with? How is it that such miraculous deeds are accomplished by his hands? Is this not the carpenter, the son of Mary, a brother of James and Joses and Judas and Simon? Are not his sisters our neighbors here?' They found him too much for them. Jesus' response to all this was: 'No man is without honor except in his native place, among his own kindred, and in his own house.' He could work no miracle there, apart from curing a few who were sick by laying hands on them, so much did their lack of faith distress him. He made the rounds of the neighboring villages instead, and spent his time teaching" (Mk 6:1-6; see also Mt 13:53-58 and Lk 4:16-30). He "could work no miracle" in his own native place because of "their lack of faith." He was too much one of them for them to be able to recognize or accept the power of God at work in him. "And he marveled because of their unbelief" (Mk 6:6—RSV).

St. Mark tells us that Jesus "marveled" because of the unbelief of his relatives, neighbors and fellow townsmen. If our recent theology of the growing human consciousness of Jesus is to be believed—if he was truly discovering as he grew who he really was and what it meant that he was one with God—we can take that word, "marveled," quite literally: He must have been surprised and deeply saddened by their reaction. St. Luke, in his description of the incident, makes very graphic the hostility and rejection which Jesus encountered: "At these words the whole audience in the synagogue was filled with indignation. They rose up and expelled him from the town, leading him to the brow of the hill on which it was built and intending to hurl him over the edge. But he went straight through their midst and walked away" (Lk 4:28-30).

I write these lines in my own hometown, in my mother's apartment. The sense of home is very strong, and the joy I have felt in returning home after several years in the Philippines is very real. I have preached and celebrated the Eucharist in my own parish, and have conducted workshops and recollections for many of my own fellow townsmen. Perhaps the very joy I have experienced in being able to share my priesthood with my own people makes even more poignant the experience of Jesus in his native place. I feel a bit spoiled, a bit guilty even, when I see how my experience contrasts with his. But even I, spoiled as I may have been, can grasp the meaning of the rejection he experienced. In far smaller ways (proportioned to my own weakness), I have experienced it too. And I have had to learn for myself that it is a very important part of my growth. Sometimes I have had much more influence on people whom I meet only on a retreat, or only through my books, than on people with whom I live and rub elbows every day. At times a parish priest or a spiritual director in a seminary may feel that his parishioners or his seminarians are the most difficult audience he has, precisely because they are constantly exposed to him, and his words of wisdom become "old hat" to them.

And religious too—it happens, I suppose, in every family, lay or religious—despite their strong sense of fraternal unity are not always very supportive of one another. We can be very demanding, very critical, taking for granted the good done by those closest to us and seemingly focusing only on what needs to be corrected or improved. Not long ago a friend, also a religious, wrote to me, and in the course of his letter commenting on the books I have written, he said: "We have so many gifted men and women in our religious communities. What a shame it is that our gifts often seem to cancel one another out!" And then he mentioned a former classmate of his who has since left religious life and has done some well-received writing as a layman. He said of this friend, "I wonder if he ever would have published, or have had such influence, if he had remained a religious." Maybe he would have done even more, but how sad it is that such a question would even be asked!

More than once, too, I have directed souls, priests or seminarians or sisters, who found great difficulty in relating to and dealing with others from their own communities who were also genuinely prayerful and committed souls. Not infrequently I have directed both of the persons in the difficult relationship, and have known both of them as deep and solid in their own spirituality. Yet somehow they were a cross for one another!

This, then, is the second kind of darkness in the marketplace of our contemplative lives: the pain and frustration that comes from failure in our outer lives, especially the failure to find God and to be Christ for those we serve and those with whom we serve. I feel sure everyone who reads these lines knows what I mean from his or her own experience. That such a darkness exists scarcely needs proof. The point we are making, however, is not that it exists but that it is a very important part of the process of purification and transformation for those called to the dark night or dry well. Let us explore, then, why and how this is so. Why not see such failure and frustration as merely our own fault, or else due to the bad will and blindness of others? Doesn't it seem too facile and fatalistic to say that this darkness is a necessary and inevitable part of our growth in holiness?

I think not. Recall that when we say "yes" to the Lord's dark night, we are really saying yes to his work of divinization in us. But we are very far from divine, and there is much in us, even after we have surrendered to love, that militates against our union with God. It would be wonderful if we could surrender once and for all, and if that were the end of pain, namely, the agony that comes from our unwillingness to really let go of our lives. If we desire to float and yet are clinging for dear life to the dock of our familiar existence, there is a tremendous release when we finally decide to let go of the dock and entrust ourselves to the water. But if we are entangled in seaweed and surrounded by flotsam, even the momentous decision to let go of the dock will not be the end of our troubles. There is no longer any dock to which we deliberately cling, but there are many things still clinging to us. Our free decision to stop clinging and to float, important as it is, does not of itself make us floaters. Our new situation can be very frustrating, indeed, particularly if there seems to be very little we can do to disentangle ourselves from the seaweed which clings to us and threatens to choke us. We have done what we can by relaxing our grip on the dock, and yet we are still not free to float!

This, of course, is where the Lord must take over the work of liberation. And he does so, as we have seen in the second part of the *Well,* precisely by the experience of the dark night. We are still entangled in many things, even when we have freely released our grip on the dock and given ourselves over to floating. The mysterious phenomenon of the readiness of the unready is, as we have seen, one of the ways in which the Lord disentangles us from the seaweed of natural values and natural ways of acting. And this happy kind of marketplace darkness would suffice to free us to float, if only we were creatures without sin. If our only problem in grasping God, at least once we had freely surrendered to his love, were the gulf between human nature and the divine, no more painful darkness would be required. But, unfortunately, we are not only creatures, we are sinners. Even when we begin to live for the Lord of love, our love still contains much that is selfish and vain. Even when we give ourselves freely to a life of service of the Lord, there is much self-will and self-seeking in our service. We find ourselves in the situation of St. Paul in

Romans when he says: "I cannot even understand my own actions. I do not do what I want to do but what I hate" (7:15). Not only is he unable to do the divine good he desires (which would be true simply because he is human and not yet divine), but he actually finds himself doing the sinful evil which he hates.

Nature can be transformed, but sin must be uprooted. And this uprooting, since the roots are so deep and widespread, inevitably involves frustration and pain. Since Jesus was the sinless one, I presume the pain he felt came not from himself but from the sinfulness of those around him, of the air he breathed. But I am not the sinless one. When I seek to serve the seminarians and help them to become good priests, there is much self-love mixed in with my apostolic zeal. When I look to my Jesuit brethren for that support and encouragement which should be part of every gospel community, my desire for approval and recognition involves much selfishness. I wish it were not so. How good it would be to do what I do purely for the Lord's glory, and to find all my joy in knowing that he is made happy by my actions. That is what I desire, and gradually—very, very gradually—it is coming to be in me. But, and this is the main point of this chapter, it is precisely the sandpaper of failure and frustration which is working this change in me.

I mentioned that the discovery of how this dark fire works its purifying effect in my heart is one of the deepest and most precious lessons of my life. If I were always successful and appreciated, my zeal for the Lord would involve much self-love. But each time I meet misunderstanding or criticism or even rejection, I am forced to ask myself why I am really working. Is it for me or for the Lord? If it is for the Lord, why am I so disturbed that my own feelings are hurt? Of course, it is easy to rationalize that his interests are mine, and thus that my distress is because he is offended. But is that really true? Have I really let him speak for himself? There is a world of difference between identifying my interests with God's (which is genuine holiness) and identifying God's interests with my own (which is the ultimate in vanity). Yet how subtle this difference is, and how easily we confuse the two in our lives.

Maybe that is why I have discovered, over the years, that the prayer I most often find myself saying goes like this: "Lord, let me be just as disturbed about this situation (or this person's behavior) as you are, no more and no less. If you are angry, let me be angry too. But if you are not disturbed, let me share your peace." It is amazing, and quite humbling, how often my disturbance simply dissolves once I say that prayer and really mean it. Humbling because it makes very clear how much of my distress comes from myself, from my own wounded self-love and my own self-righteous zeal. Only this second kind of darkness—the Calvary darkness of failure and frustration—could ever bring me to this realization. And only the Calvary darkness can eventually heal what it has brought to light.

In Chapter 4 of *When the Well Runs Dry,* I mentioned an experience I have had several times. When former students of mine at the university in Manila ask me to perform their marriages for them, there is a phrase in the marriage ceremony which strikes me and gives me pause. As I ask them to repeat the marriage vows after me, I find myself wondering if they really understand what they are saying when they commit themselves "for better or worse." I said in the *Well* that I doubt that they do. For someone 25, the phrase could only mean, "I hope and expect it will all be 'better,' but if the 'worse' comes, I will try to remain faithful to my commitment." In these days of temporary commitments and broken marriages, even that promise is a heroic one for a young person to make. But the tragedy is that our age has lost the real meaning of the "for better or worse." In a good marriage, entered into by generous people, the "worse" comes to be at least as important—and eventually even as precious—as the "better." Both are necessary to love. In the better times, we learn the joy of loving. In the worse times we learn (and there is no other way we could learn) to love unselfishly. It is the "worse" that leads us from loving to truly loving.

When I recalled this experience in the *Well,* it was to explain the value of the purifying darkness of the dry well in our interior lives. What we have discovered in this chapter is that the "worse" by which we are sanctified comes not only at the prie-dieu but also in the marketplace. In fact, as I indicated at the beginning of the chapter, the more at home we become in the inner darkness, the more important the marketplace darkness becomes to our santification. Our senses are the last part of us to be converted, and the senses are our link to the marketplace. Long after the will has surrendered to God, the senses—like some straggler in the mountains still fighting a war which ended in the capital 30 years ago—will still be resisting. If we were angels, or called to become angels, we could abandon the senses to their lost cause. We could seek to kill them or escape from them, by some extreme of desert spirituality. But we are not called to be holy angels; we are called to be holy men and women. The chapel can be truly at peace only when the marketplace has also come to peace. It is a costly struggle, but the "worse" of the marketplace is the Lord's way of bringing victory to those who desire it. And not only to them but also to the very marketplace in which they live by dying.

Six

Love to Be Overlooked

*I*f the darkness of failure and frustration is the Lord's way of disentangling us from self-love, the seaweed which ensnares us and prevents us from truly floating in him, then we can readily acknowledge its value in our lives. Not only that, but the more we grow in love, the more aware we become of this vanity so deeply rooted in us, and thus the more we desire, despite the cost in human pain, that the Lord get on with the business of purifying us, so that we can love as we are loved.

There is, however, a problem with the Calvary darkness we have been describing. It is easy to develop a martyr complex, and to become sanctimonious and self-righteous about our sufferings. At least that is how it has long seemed to me. Even in the writing of the last chapter, I sometimes had the uneasy feeling that "Calvary" was too pretentious a word to describe the experience I had in mind. I don't really believe that it is too grand, or else I would not have written as I did. But, nonetheless, the occasional uneasiness about even resurrecting my own experience was there. It is good to suffer for love, and yet something precious is lost by too much analysis or too close scrutiny. Perhaps that is why I felt Chapter 5 would be (and was) the hardest to write, even though it may well be the most important for an understanding of the place of marketplace darkness in our interior lives. The darkness of failure and frustration is perhaps the most difficult to accept and to integrate into a sound, mature spirituality. At the same time, self-pity or an exaggerated focusing on our own trials is unhealthy psychologically and harmful spiritually.

St. Teresa makes a very shrewd comment which is relevant here. In the First Mansions of *The Interior Castle,* she insists that the only sound foundation of a genuine spirituality is humility. Yet, she says, there are two ways to gain humility, one which is healthy, to keep our eyes on the Lord, and the other which is dangerous, to focus on ourselves and our own failings. "Humility must always be doing its work like a bee making its honey in the hive: Without humility all will be lost. Still, we should remember that the bee is constantly flying about from flower to flower, and in the same way, believe me, the soul must sometimes emerge from self-knowledge and soar aloft in meditation upon the greatness and majesty of its God. Doing this will help it to realize its own baseness better than thinking of its own nature . . . and, believe me, we shall reach much greater heights of virtue by thinking upon the virtue of God than if we stay in our own little plot of ground and tie ourselves down to it completely."[1] The danger of focusing on self, as she goes on to say, is that we may become timid and scrupulous and excessively self-conscious.

What Teresa says of humility applies also to the marketplace darkness of the passion of which we have been speaking. It is dangerous to focus too much on our own suffering. We may become morbid and self-pitying, joyless martyrs in and for the kingdom of God, very far from the "cheerful giver" whom the Lord loves! Then the misunderstanding and failure and frustration of which we have spoken become destructive weapons of Satan rather than the instruments of high sanctity which they should be. The fire of suffering which should temper the steel instead ends up melting the alloy which the devil has polluted.

How, then, should we act so as to foil the devil? I think the first point of advice is that we should *never seek* suffering and failure and misunderstanding, unless we are conscious of a special calling from the Lord. Even if such a calling seems present, we should not trust it without submitting it to the co-discernment of a good spiritual director. The potential dangers, as Teresa makes clear, are too great for us to act on our own. Even the great prayer, "Take and Receive," should never be understood as a request that the Lord destroy our health, or our mind, or anything else. Rather, it is a prayer that he do with them—our possessions, our faculties, our freedom—as he sees best. It is an act of trust, an affirmation that he knows and loves us more than we

---

[1] St. Teresa of Avila, *The Interior Castle,* First Mansions, Chapter 2 (pp. 37-38 in the Doubleday Peers' translation).

know and love ourselves. To trust that deeply is heroic and requires a real love-experience of God, but it is not a sanctified masochism!

Moreover, when suffering comes we should not become obsessed with it. How well I remember one sister, in the year of her golden jubilee, sharing with me the trials of her years in religious life. She was serene and joyous, and she described her experiences almost matter-of-factly. She was not looking for sympathy, but rather for reassurance that she had been on the right track all these years. She just wanted to be sure that the unusual trials she had faced were not a sign that she had somehow displeased her Lord or failed his love. How beautiful it was when she ended her sharing by saying, "My only real concern is that my life has been too easy." When I replied, in surprise, "But what about all the very difficult experiences you have been sharing with me now?" she said, "Oh, but those are very small compared to what others have to suffer! And they are nothing compared to what I deserve." I was quite certain then that her trials had been real, and equally certain that she was very close to God. Such peace and serenity could come only from him.

I think the Little Flower, St. Therese of the Child Jesus, sensed the danger of great trials. This, I believe, is what led her to her "little way." As I noted in *When the Well Runs Dry* (p. 148), she felt that this little way was appropriate for her because she was not capable of the heroic deeds of the saints; yet I believe it is really the only way, even for strong personalities like Teresa of Avila and Catherine Doherty and Charles de Foucauld. Basically the "little way" means recognizing that the Lord carries us in his arms, that our sanctification is virtually 100 percent his work. And this is a discovery which even the strongest and most talented of us must make. When we have done everything we can do, we are "only unprofitable servants," and the possession of God still eludes our grasp.

We have already discussed this at length with respect to our interior lives. It is, however, equally true in our outer, apostolic lives. And this brings me to the third point I should like to make concerning the marketplace darkness of the passion. We said that we should never seek suffering; and that, when it comes, we should not become obsessed with it but should keep our eyes on the Lord and, as far as possible, bear it with an easy grace. The further point is this: I believe there is something else which we *can seek,* and which corresponds to the little way of Therese. It is the little way of the marketplace, and it can bring the apostle all the peace and security, without danger of delusion, which Therese found in her little way. It is what I had in mind when I chose the title of this chapter: Love to Be Overlooked.

To explain further what I mean, let me share a bit of my own early experience. When I was a novice, one of the books we were given to read was a mimeographed biography of a young Jesuit who had died as a seminarian in 1930. His name was Francis X. Cullinan, and his biography had a special appeal for me since Frank Cullinan was also from Rochester. In fact, he and my father had been classmates at the old Cathedral High School and, for one year before Frank entered the Jesuits, roommates at Holy Cross

College in Worcester, Massachusetts. I had heard my dad speak of him. And when Father Forbes Monaghan, S.J., was writing his life several years earlier, he had paid us a visit to interview my father. I was intrigued with this tall Jesuit (probably the first one I had ever seen), but little did I suspect that I would one day belong to the same family as he and Frank Cullinan did.

When I read Father Monaghan's life of Frank as a novice I was excited by the link between Frank and my father—and somewhat intimidated by the austerity of Frank's life. His spirit of penance and detachment, very much the fashion in spirituality at that time, struck me in much the same way as the heroic deeds of the saints struck the young Therese: They were admirable but alarming![2] One thing, however, appealed to me powerfully in Frank Cullinan's life. It was the motto he chose for himself as the guide for his life as a Jesuit: *ama nesciri et pro nihilo reputari.* "Love to be unknown and to be accounted as nothing." This too seemed intimidating, even repugnant, to a young man of 19 seeking affection and acceptance wherever he could find them. Yet despite (or perhaps because of?) my desire to be known and

---

[2] Today I realize that much depends on the stylistic conventions of spiritual biography in a given age. Even our secular heroes, like George Washington and Abraham Lincoln, have been "demythologized" in the later writings of our anti-heroic age. But I also came to realize that Frank Cullinan died at the age of 25, almost the same age as St. Therese. Had they lived another 50 years and fulfilled their promise of sanctity, their biographers would be writing about very different, mellower and deeper personalities. Grace does not destroy nature or suspend the natural laws of personal development; it builds on, and enriches, the naturally evolving, maturing person.

loved and accounted as something, Frank's motto took deep root in me. In some dim and partly unwelcome way, I knew that he was speaking to me and that someday I would have to face up to the hidden truth which he had discovered. Now, 30 years later, the story of his austerities and even of his accidental drowning is a dim and distant memory. But his motto has taken on a deeper and deeper meaning for me as the years have passed.

"Love to be unknown and to be accounted as nothing." What does it really mean? It is a darkness, not of failure but of obscurity. It is the experience of John the Baptist, once the darling of the Jewish masses and now lying in prison eclipsed by the Lamb of God, whom he himself had pointed out to his own disciples. It is a poignant fate for one whom Jesus himself called the greatest man born of woman (Lk 7:28). Yet John himself, at the height of his influence, virtually foretold his own fate: "The testimony John gave when the Jews sent priests and Levites from Jerusalem to ask, 'Who are you?' was the direct statement, 'I am not the Messiah.' They questioned him further, 'Who, then? Elijah?' 'I am not Elijah,' he answered. 'Are you the Prophet?' 'No,' he replied. Finally they said to him: 'Tell us who you are, so that we can give some answer to those who sent us. What do you have to say for yourself?' He said, quoting the prophet Isaiah, 'I am

a voice in the desert, crying out:
Make straight the way of the Lord!'

. . .'I baptize with water. There is one among you whom you do not recognize—the one who is to come after me—the strap of whose sandal I am not worthy to unfasten' " (Jn 1:19-27). And the following day, when Jesus appeared and John recognized him and pointed him out, he said: "It is he of whom I said:

'After me is to come a man
who ranks ahead of me,
because he was before me.'

I confess I did not recognize him, though the very reason I came baptizing with water was that he might be revealed to Israel" (Jn 1:30-31). Finally, after Jesus has begun his public ministry, John the Baptist makes one final appearance in the Gospel of John before disappearing into the obscurity of prison. His disciples are disturbed that Jesus is also baptizing across the Jordan and that "everyone is flocking to him." They come to John to complain about this turn of events, but John replies to them:

"No one can lay hold on anything
unless it is given him from on high.

You yourselves are witnesses to the fact that I said: 'I am not the Messiah; I am sent before him.'

"It is the groom who has the bride.
The groom's best man
waits there listening for him
and is overjoyed to hear his voice.
That is my joy, and it is complete.
He must increase,
while I must decrease" (Jn 3:27-30).

This is the real meaning of "Love to be overlooked": not the timidity of the shrinking violet, desiring to be overlooked for fear of being embarrassed by his own inadequacy or limitations, but the joyous desire of the bridegroom's friend that all eyes be focused on the bridegroom. Because this is what I have taken Frank Cullinan's slogan to mean, I believe we can and should seek this darkness of obscurity, whereas it would usually be dangerous to seek the darkness of failure and frustration. The setting of a ring accentuates the beauty of the diamond; it does not call attention to itself. Similarly, the orchestra underscores the virtuosity of the great piano soloist; it does not compete with her for center stage. The apostle of the Lord desires to play the same role as did John the Baptist: to be the herald, the clarion voice, the friend of the bridegroom. "He must increase, while I must decrease."

Many years ago, when I was approaching ordination, a professor told us that we should so celebrate Mass that, when we left the altar, the congregation would not have noticed who the celebrant was. No gesture or mannerism should be distinctive or peculiar to us. Even then, in the days just before the liturgical reform of Vatican II, this seemed dehumanizing and mechanical to me. I felt we would be better served by having robots celebrate. Today, with the stress on personal involvement in the liturgy, such a norm would be inconceivable. The priest faces the people; the language is their own; and personal gestures like the greeting of peace are strongly recommended. Yet, there was a point to that old professor's advice, even though his way of expressing it was extreme: The priest is there not to call attention to himself but to mediate an encounter with the Lord. The people should leave the liturgy feeling that they have met the Lord (and that will involve fully the humanity of the priest), not that they have met the celebrant. If they leave agog at the virtues, even the piety, of the celebrant, something is wrong. The best man should not be the focal point of any wedding!

At the same time, the best man or bridesmaid should be fully and joyously himself or herself. If the bridesmaid hides in the pews, or blushes and titters nervously throughout the wedding, or even fails to show up out of shyness, her actions merely serve to call attention to herself. It is what my novice master used to call "humility with a hook." My modesty, my self-deprecation merely serve—if they are attention-getting devices—to keep the eyes of the audience on myself. But if I have my eyes, joyous eyes, on the Bridegroom, and if my actions and gestures complement and harmonize perfectly with his, the whole congregation will be more deeply impressed by him. It is he, and his beauty, that they will remember.

This is true not only of the priest celebrating the liturgy, but of every Christian in every marketplace event of our lives. "The fact is that whether you eat or drink—whatever you do—you should do all for the glory of God. Give no offense to Jew or Greek or to the church of God, just as I try to please all in any way I can by seeking, not my own advantage, but that of the many, that they may be saved" (1 Cor 10:31-33).

This is the very positive meaning that I have come to discover in the motto of Frank Cullinan. I think I now know why it fascinated me 30 years ago. But it is important to remember that it also repelled me then. It seemed too demanding, too negative, because I did not yet know what it meant to love Someone so much that my fulfillment and my happiness would be found in his glory and his happiness.

There was a long, dark road to be traveled from that initial "instinct" that Frank's motto was important to me. And the point of this chapter is that I could discover its real meaning and its real joy only by the experience of this third kind of marketplace darkness.

It is not natural for us to find our whole joy in someone else's glorification. The self-seeking "me" is too much alive in us. We instinctively seek recognition and appreciation for ourselves, even when we are truly committed and genuinely spiritual. But the Lord has his ways of uprooting this self-centeredness. He can bring about the marketplace events which will gradually effect the death of that self-seeking in us. We cannot do much about it ourselves, and this is why it pertains more to what John of the Cross calls the "passive purification of the soul." We can, however, desire that the Lord work it in us, and we can give him a "blank check" to place us in whatever situations are necessary to purify our love. We can pray that he use this marketplace darkness of being "overlooked," as he did with John the Baptist in prison, to center our whole life and our ministry on him. But one warning is in order here: Don't ask him unless you really mean it, because this is one prayer he will surely answer!

To Arrive Where We Started

When we left St. Martha in her kitchen, early in Chapter 3, we had a partial, initial understanding of the mysterious way the Lord was dealing with her. We said that the darkness in the kitchen after her rebuke by Jesus was really meant to be the beginning of a great change in her whole relationship to him. Far from being a disaster and a rejection as it must certainly have seemed to her at that moment, it was really a call to "come up higher," a breakthrough in Martha's transformation in God. She was called to let go of all her own ideas of what it meant to love her Lord; to discover experientially that his ways are not hers, nor his thoughts her thoughts. It was the moment when Martha began to learn the difference between working for God and doing God's work.

In the following chapters we tried to spell out in more detail the various forms this kitchen—or marketplace—darkness can and will take in the lives of all who, like Martha, come to this critical thresh-hold in their lives with God: the darkness of unpreparedness, whereby the Lord empties our mouth of our own words, in order that it may be filled with his; the Calvary darkness of rejection and misunderstanding and criticism, whereby our hearts are purified, disentangled from all the seaweed of selfishness which clings to our best thoughts and actions long after we have said our sincere "yes" to the Lord's primacy in our lives; and the painful but precious darkness of being overlooked, whereby we are truly "hidden with Christ in God" (Col 3:3) and he alone becomes the rock of our hearts and our portion forever (Ps 73:26).

The incident in Mary and Martha's house in Bethany is, to the natural eye, a trivial one with little lasting importance to Martha or to us. Small as it is in itself, however, I do not believe I have exaggerated its long-range significance for Martha and for her love-relationship to her Lord. It is the "little things," the ordinary days which often are of greatest moment in our growth. When Pope Paul VI kissed the earth of the Holy Land, and when he embraced the Orthodox Patriarch in Constantinople, his dramatic gestures had tremendous symbolic value for the mid-20th-century church. They surprised and electrified men and women accustomed to a monarchical, autocratic image of the papacy, but, had we known Paul the man better at the time, we would not have been so surprised. His lips touched the earth in Jerusalem because his knees had learned to bend long before in countless hidden ways on innumerable ordinary days. His heart had learned to embrace strangers and "schismatics" and "heretics" long before there were photographers present to record the event. For

Giovanni Battista Montini, these earlier ordinary actions on ordinary days must have seemed small indeed; only the Lord could see that they would lead to a Paul VI in Istanbul and Jerusalem. "Then the just will ask him: 'Lord, when did we see you hungry and feed you or see you thirsty and give you drink? When did we welcome you away from home or clothe you in your nakedness? When did we visit you when you were ill or in prison?' The king will answer them: 'I assure you, as often as you did it for one of my least brothers, you did it for me' " (Mt 25:37-40).

Thus small, apparently unimportant incidents can be fraught with great significance when viewed from the divine perspective. Moreover, what happens in the marketplace, even on the ordinary days, can have great interior significance. Very often mature pray-ers, those who have experienced and come to accept the interior darkness of the dry well in their prayer lives, fail to see the connection between their interior experience and the marketplace events of their day-to-day lives. Frequently the demands and frustrations of the apostolate, or of raising a family and earning a living, seem to be merely obstacles to a genuine and deep prayer life. But, if I am right in explaining the way the Lord works through these external activities and events, then we should see them quite differently. Far from being obstacles to our interior growth, they become for us the very sandpaper of our sanctification, at least as important to our growth as what happens in the solitude of formal prayer.

This means that, as our prayer life matures, the distinction between formal prayer and active service becomes blurred, if not actually erased. This, I believe, is what I have discovered in my own experience. It has given a whole new meaning to the Ignatian ideal of the "contemplative in action," called to seek God in all things. If the dry-well experience of prayer means that the Lord takes over more and more — that prayer becomes more and more, as we said in the *Well,* the time we give to the Lord to work his will in us, rather than the time when we do something— and if our description here of the blurring of the distinction between prayer and active service is also correct, then it would seem that, even in the marketplace, it will be more and more the Lord at work rather than ourselves. Even in the busiest corners of our active existence, we should begin to discover that it is he who is at work always, guiding our hand to shape events and guiding events to shape our spirits. If prayer becomes the Lord's domain, then work should also. The biblical image of the prophet now becomes symbolic of our own lives:

"Ah, LORD GOD!" I said,
"I know not how to speak; I am too young."

But the LORD answered me,

Say not, "I am too young."
To whomever I send you, you shall go;
whatever I command you, you shall speak.
Have no fear before them,
because I am with you to deliver you, says the
Lord.

Then the LORD extended his hand and touched my
mouth, saying,
See, I place my words in your mouth! (Jer 1:6-9).

As we mature in the Lord, then, the dynamic receptivity of the floater characterizes not only our prayer life but also our life of active apostolic service. The Lord is discovered to be at work in everything, and we begin to discover the beautiful depths of Jesus' claim:

"My Father is at work until now,
and I am at work as well" (Jn 5:17).

He is at work in our resting and at work in our working, and to be "contemplative" means to become ever more sensitive to the touch of his shaping hand in both work and prayer. When I was writing *When the Well Runs Dry,* it was the image of the floater in the sea of God which captured for me this sensitivity, this dynamic receptivity. As I said there (Chapter 6), the floater is not at all passive. Anyone who has ever tried to float, or to teach others to float, knows that the floater is intensely active, responding to every movement of the wind and the tide. As soon as he becomes passive, he will sink like a rock. But the activity of the floater is unlike that of the swimmer: The swimmer sets his own course and relies primarily on his own skill and muscles to get him to his goal. The floater, on the contrary, is carried by the wind and the water. He entrusts himself to forces beyond himself, and his effort is to cooperate with these forces. He is active but he is not in control. Floating may seem easy at first blush, but in the long run, I believe, it will prove much more demanding than swimming, precisely because we lose control of our own destination and destiny. The whole point of the present book is that this loss of control, this need to float, will gradually extend to the whole life—prayer *and* action—of the mature pray-er.[1]

As I have shared this manuscript with my sister and others whose judgment I value, several have said that they find it closer to their own experience, easier to identify with, than the *Well.* And this has led me to reflect on the chronology of the two darknesses—marketplace and prie-dieu—discussed in the two books. I have more or less assumed, as reflected in the order of writing, that the interior darkness of prayer would precede the various darknesses of the marketplace. Even as I was writing and before knowing the reaction of my "readers," however, I found myself reflecting that the three darknesses of this book were experienced by all human beings, whether mature pray-ers or not, in fact, whether or not God played *any* conscious part in their lives. Frustration, criticism, being overlooked and undervalued seem to be virtually universal human experiences, whether

---

[1] Since writing the *Well,* I have found another image very helpful in explaining the active receptivity of contemplative prayer: the woman's part in ballroom dancing. The image might not work very well with today's youth, since contemporary dancing leaves in doubt who, if anybody, is partnering whom! But in "the good old days" when I learned to dance, the man was supposed to lead and the woman to follow. And her role was, I think, far more crucial than his. If she tried to lead too, their push-and-shove competition would bear very little resemblance to graceful dancing. If she were merely passive, he would have to drag her about the dance floor like a sack of potatoes. But if she followed her man's lead with grace and sensitivity, she made even his gaffes look artful and graceful. Our analogy limps, of course, since the Lord, unlike the man, does not make mistakes; but still I believe it does capture nicely the meaning of active receptivity in the life of the mature pray-er.

one is a pray-er or not; indeed, whether one is a believer or not.

For some, this fact might call into question the very idea that these "darknesses" are a sign of God's working in our lives. They might well feel that I am arbitrarily "spiritualizing," giving a religious meaning to difficulties and frustrations which are a natural and universal element in human experience. But I don't think so. For me, the very universality of these marketplace darknesses is rather an indication that the Lord is at work in every human life, and that the darknesses which each person encounters are his way of teaching us—every one of us—that nothing on this earth can ever fulfill our desires and satisfy our hearts. Our hearts are restless, as St. Augustine said long ago, until they rest in him. Yet, as Francis Thompson realized in his own tormented life and expressed beautifully in *The Hound of Heaven,* most of us seem to have to try every other, lesser light in our darkness before we fall exhausted into the arms of the God who is Light.

Thus, to return to the question of chronology which my sister and others have raised, I believe that the marketplace darkness does normally precede the prie-dieu darkness of the dry well, since the former is part of every human life, whether one is a pray-er or not. But the real *meaning* of the marketplace darkness will necessarily elude us until we do begin to pray—indeed, until our prayer attains to the maturity of the dry well or the dark night. Only then will we begin to realize that the Lord has been working in our lives from the very beginning of our conscious experience. Only then will we know that our frustrations and failures are—and have always been—his way of teaching us that it is really he whom every man is seeking. Every "fondest, blindest, weakest" man and woman of us, whether we abandon ourselves to sensuality or seek escape in drink or drive ourselves to achieve fame and power by our own accomplishments, is really, deep down and whether we know it or not, seeking the Lord of love for whom our desires are made. That is true of every human being who has ever lived or ever will live. Marketplace darkness is not unique to the mature pray-er; what *is* unique to him or her is the realization of the deep meaning of this darkness.

It must be noted, though, that this realization represents a crucial moment in our growth. For it is only when we have realized what the darkness really means—whence it really comes—that we become capable of responding to it fully and lovingly. The swimmer struggling against the tide is transformed when he discovers, and accepts, the call of the tide to him, the call to float. The pull of the tide is the same after as before, but his response to it makes all the difference to the journey.

When I was a young priest celebrating daily Mass in a parish, I used to find it frustrating that so many of the congregation were elderly. I suppose I had to question the relevance of what I was doing when I saw that so many of the people I was reaching were out of the mainstream of current events. They had had their day on center stage and were now relegated to the wings. What impact could I, a young and eager priest, hope to have on the contemporary world if I seemed to spend so much time with them in the wings? Now I am older and wiser myself, and I think I understand. There are still many older people at my weekday parish liturgies, but today it makes sense to me: They are the ones who have lived long enough to discover that it is really the Lord they seek. They have, I suspect, tried to find their fulfillment in other goods; they have sought to swim through life and to achieve by their own efforts the happiness for which they were made. But now they have learned their limits, and have experienced the inevitable frustration of trying to swim for themselves.[2]

Some lucky people—the lame and the blind and the crippled in spirit, those whom the Bible calls the "anawim"—learn early in life the impossibility of swimming. But for most of us, the aging of the body and the waning of our natural powers are not only a symbol but a real cause of our letting go interiorly. At times it may happen that my seminarians, for all their generosity and zeal, scarcely understand what I am talking about when I speak the language of surrender, of floating. To them, filled as they are with the sense of their own potential for good and for happiness, such talk seems inhuman, unreal. They have "promises to keep," and I can only hope that something of my message re-echoes in them many years hence, when their promises lie broken at their feet.

---

[2] I think I also understand now the reverence for age and the aged for which Oriental cultures, perhaps especially the Chinese, are famous. Age brings wisdom for those who are open to growth. And wisdom, theologically, is the "relish for the things of God." A person can age physically without ever really becoming wise. But one who ages gracefully inevitably discovers, by long experience and by trial and error, that only the Lord can bring secure peace to these restless hearts of ours.

Like Francis Thompson, it seems we have to try for ourselves every other avenue to happiness before we can accept the fact that only the Lord can fulfill us. How fortunate, by contrast, are they—my congregation of old-folks—who have lived long enough to discover and accept the necessity of floating! How good is this God of ours, who waits until our foolishness has run its course! May his patience always outlast our stubbornness. And may we, who have learned even a little about the joy of floating, reflect this joy in our faces and in our lives. May we be sacraments for the swimmers around us, for whom the Lord of love waits so patiently.